Fallen Angels and the Fire From Heaven

Fallen Angels and the Fire From Heaven

The War For Humanity- A Call to Arms

By Drew Allen

Fallen Angels and the Fire From Heaven
© 2025 Drew Allen. All rights reserved.

ISBN: 979-8-9934737-2-7 (eBook/Electronic Media)
ISBN: 979-8-9934737-3-4 (Paperback)
ISBN: 979-8-9934737-8-9 (Hardcover)

First Edition (Edited)
Printed in the United States of America

Cover design by Drew Allen
Interior design by Drew Allen

Preface

In my previously-written book, "Fallen Angels & Grey Skies – Aliens, Chemtrails and the War for Humanity", I explored the foundations of this conflict... the serpent's whisper in the garden of Eden, the oath of the Watchers (the fallen angels), and the corruption of the flesh that set humanity on a path of estrangement from GOD. That book laid some groundwork, and I strongly suggest you read it. However, this book is not a just a continuation of that one. It stands on its own, carrying the story forward into its escalation. Further, this is an edited version, and I made changes after feedback that parts needed more clarity.

In this book, the focus is not only on the origins of the story about the spiritual war in which we have always been engaged, but on the war as it unfolds now. We trace the machinery of control as it fractures time, language, and reality itself. We uncover the councils that still convene in secrecy, the custodians who enforce silence, and the rituals of pharmakeia and war that masquerade as progress. We follow detailed examples of the remnant who resist... not with weapons of steel, but with those of remembrance, covenant, and light.

This book is not just entertainment. It is an alarm and a summons. It is not a story of despair. It is a call to arms. Not a call to violence, but vigilance and covenant. It is my hope that it illuminates and helps stir the inner flame of those who must endure.

- Drew Allen

Table of Contents

Introduction

History does not follow a straight line. It is a battlefield of memory that is written, erased, and rewritten again. Beneath the ruins of empires and the fragments of myth lies a deeper story: one of rebellion and remembrance, of forbidden knowledge and hidden preservation.

This book begins with a conviction: that the war for humanity is real. It began with an oath sworn in defiance, when heavenly beings (the fallen angles, the "Watchers") descended and bound themselves to corruption. It continued in the rise of hybrid Kenite rulers, councils of secrecy, and rituals of war and pharmakeia that has cloaked estrangement from GOD as progress. And it has never ended. The very same forces that once whispered in caves now legislate in boardrooms, manipulate through technologies, and fracture memory itself.

This is a chronicle of hope, not despair. Just as estrangement from GOD has endured, so too has HIS remnant. Across every age, there have been preservers of memory, such as prophets, scribes, reformers, and ordinary men and women who refused to forget. Their remembrance is not nostalgia; it is resistance. Their covenant is not ritual; it is light.

Here, we trace the escalation of this war. We uncover the machinery of control that fractures time, language, and reality. We expose the councils that still convene in darkness. We confront the great deception that seeks to erase memory and enslave humanity. And, too, we follow the remnant, those who wield remembrance as a weapon, who gather at the table as covenant with GOD, who shine light into the machinery of estrangement from HIM.

The fire from heaven is not metaphor. It is judgment, vindication, and commissioning. It is the moment when deception collapses, when the remnant's altar is answered, and when covenant is confirmed before the nations.

This book is written for those who sense that history is deeper than textbooks admit, that myth is not fantasy but memory, and that the war between covenant and control is not yet finished. It is both a warning and a commissioning: a warning of the systems that seek to erase, and a call for you to join HIS remnant who preserve, resist, and endure.

The war for humanity is here. Their net is collapsing. The fire will soon fall. Are you ready?

Part I -
Descent and Control

Chapter 1 - The Oath on Hermon

"They swore together and bound themselves by oath."
- *Book of Enoch (Ethiopic tradition)*

On Mount Hermon, two hundred angels descended and sealed their rebellion against GOD with an oath. This was no passing desire but a covenant of corruption. Their pact bound heaven's rebels to earth's daughters, inaugurating a system of estrangement from GOD that would echo through every age. To understand the war that continues to this day, one must return to the mountain where rebellion became ritual.

The Mountain of the Oath

Mount Hermon rises as a sentinel on the northern frontier of Israel, and is a place of snow-capped peaks and ancient shrines. In biblical memory, it is both a boundary and a threshold... a liminal space where heaven and earth seem to touch. It was here, according to 1 Enoch, that two hundred celestial beings (the fallen angels) descended. Led by the fallen angel Semjaza, they swore an oath that would alter the course of history.

The text records their hesitation: that none of them wished to act alone, fearing the weight of their transgression. But together, they bound themselves by mutual imprecations, swearing that if judgment fell, it would fall on all of them alike. This was not merely rebellion; it was fraternity. It was the first covenant of corruption; a pact sealed not in obedience but in estrangement from GOD.

A Counter-Covenant

The oath on Hermon is best understood as a counterfeit covenant. Where Sinai would later bind Israel to GOD in law and remembrance, the oath at Mount Hermon bound the Watchers (the fallen angels) to rebellion and erasure. Both events took place on mountains, both involved oaths, both shaped generations. But one covenant preserved memory of GOD and GOD's plan; the other sought to erase it.

This inversion is central to the war of history. The Watchers did not simply fall; they organized. They did not merely transgress; they institutionalized their rebellion. Their oath was the foundation of a system that would manifest in forbidden knowledge, hybrid offspring, and the machinery of control that still governs the world today.

The Forbidden Teachings

Each Watcher brought a gift to mankind... knowledge withheld by GOD for a reason, knowledge that in the wrong hands became corruption. Azazel taught metallurgy and weaponry, turning creation into instruments of war. Semjaza taught enchantments and sorcery, corrupting the unseen. Penemue taught writing, not as remembrance of GOD and HIS LAW, but as manipulation. Others taught astrology, root-cutting, and the courses of the heavens.

These were not neutral skills. They were accelerants of estrangement from GOD. They gave humanity tools without covenant, power without purpose, knowledge without wisdom. The oath on Hermon was not only about desire; it was about the transmission of forbidden arts that would fracture creation itself.

The Birth of the Nephilim

From this oath came offspring... the Nephilim... giants and tyrants who devoured the earth. They were the children on the fallen angels who mated with human females. They were described as "men of renown," but their renown was terror. They consumed resources, enslaved populations, and turned creation into chaos.

Their very existence was a corruption of flesh, a violation of the created order.

The Nephilim were not merely large in stature; they were large in appetite. They embodied the serpent's legacy: knowledge weaponized, covenant abandoned, power divorced from purpose. Their presence was the visible fruit of the oath sworn on Mount Hermon.

The Judgment Pronounced

The oath could not stand unchallenged. According to 1 Enoch, GOD sent the archangels to intervene. Michael, Raphael, Gabriel, and Uriel were dispatched to bind the Watchers, destroy their offspring, and warn Noah (Noe) of the coming Flood. Hermon's oath was answered by heaven's decree: rebellion would be restrained, corruption erased, memory preserved through GOD's judgment.

Yet the oath's legacy endured. The Watchers were supposedly bound, but their teachings survived. The Nephilim perished, but their spirits remained as demons, since GOD had not made a place for spirits such as theirs. The systems of estrangement from GOD adapted, resurfacing in new forms across ages. Mount Hermon was not the end of rebellion; it was its beginning.

Modern Echoes of Hermon

The oath on Hermon is not ancient myth alone. Its patterns echo in some modern fraternities, some secret societies, and certain councils that bind themselves by oaths of secrecy and allegiance. The Watchers' counterfeit covenant sometimes finds new expression in organizations that promise enlightenment but deliver control, that offer knowledge but demand silence.

The rituals may change, but the structure remains: an oath, a fraternity, a transmission of forbidden knowledge, and a system of estrangement. Hermon's shadow stretches into laboratories, legislatures, and digital networks. The war that began on that mountain continues still.

Conclusion of Chapter 1

The oath on Hermon was the first organized rebellion, the first fraternity of estrangement. It inverted covenant, corrupted flesh, and institutionalized forbidden knowledge. Its legacy is visible in every age where power is divorced from purpose, where knowledge is weaponized, and where secrecy binds men to darkness.

To begin this book with Mount Hermon is to begin where the war began in earnest. For if we are to understand the machinery of control, the rituals of war, and the fracturing of reality, we must first understand the oath that set them in motion.

Chapter 2 - Machinery of Control

"They call it peace, when there is no peace."
- Jeremiah 6:14

The Watchers' rebellion did not end with corrupted flesh; it became a system. Their oath on Mount Hermon birthed not only giants but structures... scaffolds of control that masqueraded as order.

What began as forbidden knowledge became some of the institutions, rituals, and technologies that promised progress while binding humanity in obedience. To see the war clearly, one must recognize the machinery that hums beneath every empire.

From Oath to Infrastructure

The oath on Hermon was not a private sin but a public system. The Watchers institutionalized their rebellion, embedding it into the very fabric of civilization. Metallurgy became not only weapons, but the basis of whole economies. Writing became not only remembrance but propaganda. Sorcery became not only enchantment but policy. What began as forbidden arts became the scaffolding of empire.

The serpent's whisper, "ye shall be as gods", was translated into infrastructure. Humanity was offered power apart from GOD's covenant, and in accepting it, built systems that enslaved rather than liberated. The machinery of control was born.

The Architecture of Estrangement

Every empire carries the same blueprint:
- Centralized Authority- kings, councils, or corporations that claim divine mandate.
- Economic Nets- currencies, debts, and markets that bind populations in dependence.
- Military Apparatus- armies and weapons that sanctify violence as order.
- Religious Facades- temples, shrines, or ideologies that mask control as worship.
- Information Systems- scribes, schools, and media that shape memory itself.

These are not neutral structures. They are the Watchers' architecture, designed to replace covenant with compliance. The machinery of control is not accidental; it is ritualized estrangement.

The Illusion of Progress

Civilization often cloaks itself in the language of advancement. New tools, new laws, new technologies are hailed as progress. Yet beneath the surface, the same patterns repeat: debt replaces freedom, surveillance replaces trust, and compliance replaces covenant.

The prophets of Israel saw this clearly. Jeremiah condemned those who cried "peace" while building scaffolds of oppression. Amos denounced those who trampled the poor while singing hymns. The machinery of control has always worn the mask of progress.

Ancient Parallels

- Egypt built monuments to gods and kings while enslaving populations.
- Babylon exalted its ziggurats while erasing covenantal memory.
- Rome offered roads and order while crucifying dissenters.

Each empire claimed to bring light, but each was powered by the same machinery: centralized authority, economic nets, military might, religious facades, and information control. The Watchers' oath echoed in every stone laid, every law written, every coin minted.

Modern Manifestations

The machinery of control did not vanish with Rome. It adapted. Today, it hums in:

- Global finance systems that bind nations in debt.
- Digital surveillance that monitors every transaction and word.
- Pharmaceutical dependence that sanctifies pharmakeia as progress.
- Media empires that rewrite memory in real time.
- Technocratic councils that legislate without covenant.

The same blueprint persists, only clothed in new technologies. The fallen angels' oath on Mount Hermon still whispers in boardrooms, laboratories, and networks.

The Ritual of Compliance

Control is not maintained by force alone; it is ritualized. Citizens are taught to pledge allegiance, to repeat slogans, to consume narratives. These rituals are not neutral. They are liturgies of estrangement, designed to bind populations in obedience.

The machinery of control thrives on participation. Virtually every oath sworn to empire, every ritual of compliance, every silence in the face of corruption strengthens its scaffolding. The war is not only external; it is internal, fought in the choices of memory and allegiance.

The Remnant's Resistance

Yet even within empires, the remnant endures. Israel preserved GOD's covenant under Pharaoh. The early Christians remembered their faith under Rome's depredations. Hidden faithful carried manuscripts through the fires of Babylon and later there were the inquisitions of the Catholic church in Europe.

The machinery of control is vast, but it is not invincible. Its weakness is truth. Its enemy is remembrance. Its collapse begins when the remnant refuses to comply, when memory is preserved, when covenant is chosen over convenience.

Conclusion of Chapter 2

The machinery of control is the Watchers' most enduring legacy. It is the system that cloaks estrangement as progress, that binds humanity in obedience while promising freedom. From Mount Hermon to Babylon to the digital age, its scaffolding remains the same.

To see the war clearly, one must recognize the machinery beneath the surface. For only then can the remnant resist, remembering that covenant is not a system but a relationship, not machinery but light.

Chapter 3 -
Custodians of Flesh

"All flesh had corrupted his way upon the earth."
- Genesis 6:12

The Watchers' oath did not remain abstract. It took form in bodies, in bloodlines, in corrupted flesh that carried estrangement from GOD across generations. Giants once walked the earth, but when their bodies perished, their legacy endured in subtler forms, as we will soon discuss... hybrid lineages, altered genomes, and vessels prepared for occupation. To understand the persistence of rebellion, one must see how flesh itself became a ledger of corruption.

Flesh as Battlefield

Genesis 6 declares that "all flesh had corrupted his way upon the earth." This corruption was not merely moral but biological. The Watchers' union with human women produced the Nephilim, hybrids who embodied estrangement from GOD in their very DNA. Flesh became the battlefield of rebellion, the medium through which corruption was transmitted.

The serpent's whisper in Eden had targeted the mind; the oath on Mount Hermon targeted the body. Together, they ensured that estrangement from GOD was not only remembered, but inherited.

The Nephilim Legacy

The Nephilim were described as "mighty men of old, men of renown" (Genesis 6:4). Yet their renown was terror. They consumed resources, enslaved populations, and turned creation into chaos. When the Flood erased their bodies, their spirits remained... restless, bodiless, and hungry. GOD had no place for these spirits, for HE had not created them. These became known as the demons of later ages, seeking embodiment wherever they could find it.

Thus, the corruption of flesh did not end with the Flood. It adapted. The Nephilim's spirits became parasites, and their bloodlines reemerged in hybridized forms. Flesh remained the chosen vessel of estrangement from GOD.

Hybrid Lineages

Scripture hints at lineages that carried corruption beyond the Flood. The Anakim, Rephaim, and Zamzummim are described as giants inhabiting Canaan (Deuteronomy 2–3). Goliath of Gath is but one infamous example. These lineages suggest that hybrid blood survived, whether through hidden vessels, subterranean refuges, or spiritual possession.

The Kenites (descendants of Cain) also appear as ambiguous custodians… smiths and scribes who preserved fragments of forbidden knowledge. Their survival across ages suggests that corruption was not eradicated but preserved in bloodlines and crafts.

Flesh as Custodianship

The Watchers' strategy was simple: corrupt the vessel, and you corrupt the covenant with GOD. If covenant is transmitted through generations, then altering flesh alters memory itself. Hybrid lineages became custodians of estrangement, carrying rebellion in their very bodies.

This strategy persists. Modern manipulation of flesh (through genetic engineering, pharmaceuticals, and biotechnologies) echoes the Watchers' ancient tactics. The battlefield of flesh has never been abandoned.

Mythic Parallels

Cultures across the world preserve memory of hybrid custodians:

- Greek mythology speaks of demigods, born of gods and mortals, who wielded great power but often brought ruin.
- Mesopotamian epics describe Apkallu, semi-divine sages who taught forbidden arts.
- Mesoamerican traditions recall feathered serpents and hybrid rulers who claimed descent from the gods.
- Hindu texts speak of nagas and asuras, beings who mingled with humanity and altered destinies.

These myths are not isolated. They are echoes of the same memory: flesh corrupted, hybrids enthroned, estrangement from GOD institutionalized.

Modern Echoes

Today, the custodians of flesh wear new disguises:
- Genetic engineering promises cures but risks corruption of the created order.
- Transhumanist movements seek to merge flesh with machine, severing humanity from covenant.
- Pharmaceutical dependence alters body and mind, binding populations in chemical obedience.
- Biometric surveillance reduces flesh to data, commodifying the body as a tool of control.

Each of these echoes the Watchers' strategy: to make flesh the medium of estrangement, to turn the body into a ledger of rebellion.

The Remnant's Purity

Against this corruption, scripture preserves the image of Noah: "perfect in his generations" (Genesis 6:9). This phrase suggests not only moral integrity but genetic wholeness. Noah's family carried uncorrupted flesh, preserving GOD's covenant through the Flood.

The remnant today is called to a similar purity... not in isolation from the world, but in resistance to its corruptions. To preserve covenant is to guard flesh, to resist manipulation, to remember that the body is not a vessel for estrangement but a temple of the Spirit.

Conclusion of Chapter 3

The custodians of flesh are the Watchers' most enduring strategy. By corrupting the vessel, they ensured that estrangement would be inherited, not merely remembered. From Nephilim giants to hybrid lineages to modern genetic manipulations, the war has always been written in flesh.

Yet the remnant endures. Just as Noah (Noe) preserved covenant through purity of generations, so too can the faithful resist corruption today. For flesh is not merely a battlefield; it is also a temple. And in that temple, covenant still dwells.

Chapter 4 - Hybrid Councils

"The kings of the earth set themselves, and the rulers take counsel together, against the LORD, and against his anointed."
- Psalm 2:2

The oath on Hermon birthed not only corrupted flesh but corrupted governance. From the shadows of antiquity to the halls of modern power, councils have convened... hybrid in blood, hybrid in allegiance, hybrid in purpose. These assemblies are not merely political; they are ritual. They are the continuation of the unholy oath at Mount Hermon, the institutional face of estrangement from GOD. To understand the persistence of this rebellion, one must trace the councils that rule from beneath the surface of the world.

The Archetype of the Council

From the beginning, rebellion has been collective. The Watchers swore their oath together, binding themselves in fraternity. The Nephilim ruled not as solitary tyrants but as dynasties. The custodians of flesh did not act alone but formed networks of bloodlines and alliances.

This pattern persists: estrangement thrives in councils. Where covenant to GOD gathers the faithful in remembrance, estrangement from HIM gathers rulers in secrecy. The council is the counterfeit of fellowship. It is a table where rebellion is planned, where secrecy is enforced, where allegiance is sworn not to GOD but to power.

Ancient Councils of Rebellion

- The Divine Council of the Nations: Deuteronomy 32:8-9 hints that the nations were divided under the authority of lesser beings, while Israel was preserved as YHWH's portion. These councils of "gods" became custodians of estrangement, ruling nations in rebellion.
- The Sanhedrins of Empire: Babylon, Persia, and Rome each convened councils of priests, scribes, and rulers who enforced imperial cults. Their decrees were not merely political but spiritual, binding populations in ritualized obedience.
- The Watchers' Legacy: Extra-biblical traditions describe subterranean assemblies where hybrid rulers preserved forbidden knowledge, passing it through generations. These were not myths of democracy but memories of occult governance.

The Hybrid Nature of Power

The councils of estrangement are hybrid in three ways:
1. Hybrid in Blood- lineages that trace descent from Nephilim, Anakim, or other corrupted lines, claiming divine right to rule.
2. Hybrid in Allegiance- rulers who serve both earthly thrones and unseen powers, mediating between human populations and spiritual rebels.
3. Hybrid in Purpose- councils that blend politics, religion, and sorcery into a single apparatus of control.

This hybridity is their strength and it is also their curse. It allows them to endure across ages, but it also reveals their counterfeit nature. They are neither fully human nor fully divine, neither covenantal nor free.

The Secrecy of the Council

Psalm 2 describes rulers who "take counsel together" against the LORD. Their strength lies in secrecy. Oaths of silence, veils of ritual, and layers of hierarchy ensure that their true allegiance remains hidden.

This secrecy is itself a ritual. Just as the Watchers swore their oath on Mount Hermon, so too do modern councils bind themselves by secrecy. The oath is the lifeblood of estrangement, ensuring that rebellion is preserved across generations.

Mythic and Cultural Echoes

- Greek Boule and Roman Senate: Though celebrated as democratic, these councils often served elite families with hybrid claims of divine descent.
- Mesoamerican Priest-Kings: Councils of rulers and shamans claimed to mediate between gods and men, enforcing rituals of blood sacrifice.
- Some Medieval Orders: Some secret fraternities and knightly orders often blended Christian imagery with forbidden esoteric practices, preserving hybrid allegiances.
- Some Modern Secret Societies: From clandestine (illegitimate) Masonic lodges to globalist councils, the pattern persists… oaths, secrecy, ritual, and influence beyond the public eye.

Each culture remembers the same archetype: councils that claim enlightenment but enforce estrangement from GOD.

Modern Manifestations of Hybrid Councils

Today, the councils of estrangement wear new masks:
- Political Alliances- summits and think tanks where unelected elites shape global policy.
- Financial Networks- central banks and transnational corporations that dictate economies.
- Scientific Boards- councils that legislate biotechnology, pharmakeia, and genetic manipulation.
- Digital Consortia- groups that control information, censor dissent, and rewrite memory.

These councils are hybrid not only in membership but in function. They blend governance, economy, science, and media into a single apparatus of control. Their rituals are not sacrifices on altars but signatures on treaties, patents, and algorithms.

The Remnant's Counter-Council

Against these councils stands another: the fellowship of the faithful. Where estrangement often gathers in clandestine secrecy, covenant gathers in remembrance. Where hybrid councils enforce silence, the remnant proclaims truth. Where rulers conspire against the LORD, the remnant kneels before HIM.

The early church understood this. They met in homes, broke bread, and remembered. Their fellowship was a counter-council, a table of resistance against Rome's senate and Sanhedrin alike. The same pattern endures today: every gathering of the faithful is a council of light against the councils of estrangement.

There are also organizations of good and light that are not clandestine. Some of these are thousands of years old. They are in pitch battle with the evil enemy today, and we will not talk of some of them in this book, and save that discussion for later.

Conclusion of Chapter 4

The hybrid councils are the institutional face of rebellion. From Mount Hermon to Babylon to the digital age, rulers have conspired together, binding themselves by secrecy and oath. Their power is hybrid, their allegiance divided, their purpose estranged.

Yet their councils are not the final word. Against them stands another table... the covenantal fellowship of GOD's remnant. Where estrangement conspires in darkness, remembrance gathers in light. And in the end, it is not the councils of rebellion that endure, but the council of the one true GOD.

Chapter 5 - Ritual of War

"Ye lust, and have not: ye kill, and desire to have, and cannot obtain: ye fight and war, yet ye have not, because ye ask not."
- James 4:2

War is never only about territory. It is ritual... a liturgy of blood and fire, sanctified by rulers and priests, engineered by councils, and disguised as necessity. From the Watchers' teachings of weaponry to the empires that rose on sacrifice, war has always been an altar as much as a battlefield. To understand the machinery of estrangement from GOD, one must see war not as accident but as ritual.

War as Liturgy

The Watchers taught men to forge swords, shields, and breastplates (1 Enoch 8:1). The leader of the fallen angels, Azazel, gave instruction that was not neutral technology; it was the sanctification of violence. War became a liturgy... a repeated act of bloodshed that bound nations in cycles of sacrifice.

Every battle is framed as necessity, but beneath the rhetoric lies ritual. The spilling of blood, the burning of cities, the offering of sons and daughters to the fire. These are not only strategies of conquest but ceremonies of estrangement from GOD.

Ancient Wars as Sacrifice

In each of these cases, war was not merely political. It was ritualized violence, sanctified as worship.

- Canaanite Rituals: Archaeological evidence suggests that child sacrifice accompanied warfare, sanctifying battles as offerings to Molech and Baal.
- Assyrian Campaigns: Kings recorded their conquests as offerings to their gods, inscribing victories on stelae as liturgical acts.
- Roman Triumphs: Victorious generals paraded captives through Rome, offering them as sacrifices to Jupiter.
- Aztec Warfare: Battles were fought not only for territory but to capture victims for ritual sacrifice, feeding the gods with blood.

The Watchers' Legacy in Warfare

The oath on Mount Hermon institutionalized war as ritual. By teaching metallurgy and enchantments, the Watchers ensured that violence would become systemic. War was no longer spontaneous conflict; it was engineered, ritualized, and sanctified.

This legacy persists. Every empire has used war as a tool of control, a ritual of pruning populations, resetting economies, and consolidating power. War is estrangement from GOD disguised as necessity.

The Economic Dimension of War

War is also an economic ritual.
- Spoils of Conquest: Ancient empires enriched themselves through plunder, sanctifying theft as divine right.
- Debt and Reconstruction: Modern wars leave nations indebted, rebuilding under the control of financiers.
- Military-Industrial Complex: In the modern age, war itself has become an industry, feeding economies through perpetual conflict.

The ritual of war is not only blood but coin. It is sacrifice on the altar of economy, binding nations in cycles of debt and dependence.

The Psychological Dimension of War

War also reshapes memory.
- Propaganda sanctifies violence as patriotism.
- Monuments enshrine sacrifice as glory.

- Education retells battles as noble necessity.

These are not neutral acts. They are rituals of remembrance inverted... memory weaponized to preserve estrangement from GOD. Where covenant calls us to remember GOD's acts of deliverance, empire calls us to remember its wars as salvation.

Modern Rituals of War

Today, the ritual persists in new forms:
- World Wars as pruning events, resetting global orders.
- Cold War as ritualized fear, sustaining economies of armament.
- Endless Conflicts in the Middle East as perpetual sacrifice zones, feeding industries and ideologies alike.
- Cyber and Information Wars as new liturgies, fought not with swords but with data, yet still sanctified as necessity.
- The altar has changed, but the ritual remains. War is still engineered, still sanctified, still offered as sacrifice.

The Remnant's Resistance

Against the ritual of war stands GOD's remnant. Scripture calls the faithful to beat swords into plowshares (Isaiah 2:4), to resist the sanctification of violence. The early church refused to serve in Rome's legions, recognizing war as ritual estrangement. GOD calls HIS people to war... not man.

The remnant today resists not by armies but by memory. To remember GOD's covenant is to refuse the liturgy of man's wars, to see through the propaganda, to expose the altar beneath the battlefields.

Conclusion of Chapter 5

War is not accident but ritual. It is the Watchers' liturgy, sanctified by councils, engineered by empires, and disguised as necessity. From ancient sacrifices to modern conflicts, the pattern remains: blood spilled as offering, economies reset as worship, memory reshaped as obedience.

Yet GOD's remnant endures. Against the ritual of war stands the covenant of peace. Against the altar of violence stands the table of remembrance. And in the end, it is not war that prevails, but GOD, and HE alone truly rules.

Chapter 6 -
Sorcery of Pharmakeia

"For by thy sorceries were all nations deceived."
- Revelation 18:23

The Watchers' oath corrupted flesh not only through hybrid lineages but through substances... potions, enchantments, and pharmakeia. What began as forbidden arts in the days of Enoch has resurfaced in laboratories, patents, and prescriptions. Pharmakeia is not merely medicine; it is sorcery disguised as science, dependency sanctified as progress. The very definition of the word pharmakeia is a Greek word that translates to "sorcery" or "witchcraft". To understand the war that continues, one must see how the corruption of flesh has been ritualized through pharmakeia.

The Ancient Roots of Pharmakeia

The Greek word pharmakeia appears in the New Testament, translated as "sorcery" (Galatians 5:20; Revelation 9:21; 18:23). It refers not only to potions but to the manipulation of body and mind through substances. In antiquity, pharmakeia was inseparable from enchantment. Herbs, metals, and elixirs were combined with incantations to alter perception, induce dependency, and open gateways to spiritual influence.

The Watchers taught these arts. 1 Enoch records that the fallen angel Semjaza and his companions revealed root-cuttings, enchantments, and the use of herbs. These were not gifts of healing but tools of corruption. Pharmakeia was the counterfeit of GOD's covenantal anointing... a ritual that bound flesh not to GOD but to estrangement from HIM.

Pharmakeia as Control

Pharmakeia is not neutral. It is a system of control:
- Dependency: Substances create reliance, binding individuals to suppliers and systems.
- Alteration: Potions and drugs alter perception, weakening discernment and memory.
- Ritualization: The use of substances becomes liturgy, repeated acts that bind body and spirit.

In every age, pharmakeia has been weaponized. From ancient temples to modern clinics, the pattern remains: substances offered as salvation, dependency disguised as healing.

Biblical Warnings

Scripture consistently condemns pharmakeia:
- Galatians 5:20 lists it among the works of the flesh, alongside idolatry and witchcraft.
- Revelation 9:21 laments that humanity "repented not of their murders, nor of their sorceries."
- Revelation 18:23 declares that Babylon deceived all nations by pharmakeia.

These warnings are not metaphorical. They reveal pharmakeia as a global system of deception, a counterfeit salvation that ensnares nations.

Historical Echoes

Each culture preserved the same memory: pharmakeia as sorcery, substances as gateways to estrangement.

- Egyptian Temples: Priests mixed potions with incantations, binding worshippers in cycles of dependency.
- Greek Mystery Cults: Initiates consumed hallucinogens to encounter gods, mistaking altered perception for revelation.
- Medieval Alchemy: Sorcerers sought elixirs of life, blending science and occultism in pursuit of forbidden knowledge.

Modern Pharmakeia

Today, pharmakeia wears the mask of science:

- Pharmaceutical Empires: Corporations patent substances that create dependency, profiting from perpetual treatment rather than cure.
- Biotechnology: Genetic manipulation alters flesh at the cellular level, echoing the Watchers' corruption.
- Psychopharmacology: Drugs alter perception and behavior, reshaping identity itself.
- Global Mandates: Populations are compelled into ungodly compliance through medical decrees, binding nations in pharmakeia's net.

What was once whispered in temples is now legislated in boardrooms. Pharmakeia has become global policy.

The Spell of Progress

Pharmakeia thrives because it cloaks itself in the language of progress. Healing, safety, and advancement are invoked as justifications. Yet beneath the rhetoric lies the same pattern: dependency, alteration, and control.

The spell is powerful because it appeals to fear. Fear of sickness, fear of death, fear of exclusion... these are the levers by which pharmakeia binds populations. The promise of salvation through substances is the oldest lie in a new bottle.

The Remnant's Response

Against pharmakeia stands the covenant of healing. Scripture presents GOD as healer: "I am the LORD that healeth thee" (Exodus 15:26). True healing restores covenant with GOD, while pharmakeia severs it.

The remnant resists by remembering:
- That the body is a temple, not a vessel for estrangement from GOD.
- That healing comes from covenant, not from sorcery.
- That dependency on GOD is freedom, while dependency on pharmakeia is bondage.

The remnant's task is not to reject all medicine but to discern the difference between healing and sorcery, between covenantal care and pharmakeia's spell.

Conclusion of Chapter 6

Pharmakeia is the Watchers' sorcery reborn. It is the corruption of flesh through substances, the binding of nations through dependency, the deception of progress cloaking estrangement. From ancient temples to modern laboratories, the pattern remains.

Yet the remnant endures. Against pharmakeia stands the covenant of healing, the remembrance of GOD as physician, the refusal to bow to sorcery disguised as science. For in the end, it is not pharmakeia that heals the nations, but the leaves of the tree of life (Revelation 22:2).

Part II -
Remnant and Resistance

Chapter 7 -
Remnant of Light

"A remnant shall return, even the remnant of Jacob, unto the mighty GOD."
- Isaiah 10:21

Across every age of estrangement from GOD, a remnant has endured. While empires rose and fell, while councils conspired in darkness, while pharmakeia bound nations in deception, there were always those who remembered. Some were individuals, some were families, some were entire bloodlines who carried GOD's covenant through centuries. Others gathered in secret fellowships, organizations that have fought for millennia ... some known, others hidden. To understand the hope that counters estrangement, one must see the remnant: the quiet preservers of covenant, the keepers of memory, the bearers of light.

The Pattern of the Remnant

Scripture consistently preserves the theme of the remnant:
- Noah (Noe) and his family preserved covenant through the Flood.
- Lot was delivered from Sodom's destruction.
- Elijah (Eliyahu) was reminded that seven thousand had not bowed to Baal (1 Kings 19:18).
- Israel itself was preserved through exile, a remnant returning to rebuild Jerusalem.

The remnant is not an accident of history but a divine pattern. When estrangement saturates the world, GOD preserves a remnant to carry memory forward.

Bloodlines of Resistance

Beyond individuals, there have been family bloodlines that carried covenantal memory across generations. These families, scattered across nations, became bulwarks against estrangement from GOD. They preserved scripture, guarded traditions, and resisted corruption even when surrounded by empires of darkness.

Throughout history, these bloodlines have fought evil and served mankind. They are not exalted in chronicles, but their influence is felt in the survival of truth, the preservation of texts, and the endurance of covenantal traditions.

Examples include:
- The Coptic Christian families of Egypt - enduring centuries of conquest and cultural pressure, they preserved liturgy in the Coptic language and maintained covenantal

witness through family continuity, even when churches were destroyed or suppressed.

- The Jewish families of Yemen - carrying Torah traditions in isolation, they safeguarded covenantal practices despite poverty, persecution, and forced conversions, proving that covenantal memory can survive in the harshest conditions.
- The Armenian families of Anatolia - enduring waves of violence and displacement, they preserved covenantal identity through oral tradition, hymnody, and family worship, ensuring that memory survived even genocide.
- The Nestorian Christian lineages of Persia and Central Asia - scattered across trade routes, they carried scripture and covenantal teaching into distant lands, preserving memory even as empires sought to erase them.

These families exist even today... watched, studied, and manipulated by estranged powers who seek to corrupt or extinguish them. Yet despite surveillance and pressure, they endure, carrying light in their very lineage.

Secret Fellowships of the Remnant

Alongside families, there have been remnant organizations... fellowships that have endured for thousands of years. Some are known to the masses, others whispered in history and legend, and still others remain hidden, their existence preserved only in fragments of testimony and rumor.

Some known examples include:
- The Bogomils of the Balkans - a fellowship that resisted both empire and church, preserving alternative

testimony in secrecy until their suppression, showing how hidden groups can endure for generations.

- The Moravian Brethren - a fellowship that arose in hidden communities, later sparking global missionary movements, proving that small circles of remembrance can reshape history.
- The Celtic monastic networks - scattered across Ireland and Scotland, they preserved scripture and covenantal teaching in remote monasteries, resisting both Viking raids and imperial assimilation.
- The Ethiopian monastic fellowships - guardians of ancient texts and traditions, they preserved covenantal witness in mountain monasteries, ensuring continuity even when surrounded by hostile powers.

Many of these groups fought in silence, preserving archives, resisting councils, and shielding bloodlines. They were not perfect, nor immune to infiltration, but their persistence testifies to the endurance of covenant with God. Their secrecy was not ambition but survival. It was a way to preserve light when estrangement sought to extinguish it.

Light in Darkness

The remnant is described as light. "Ye are the light of the world" (Matthew 5:14). Light exposes what darkness conceals, reveals what estrangement erases, and guides those who wander.

The remnant's light is not their own but covenantal. It is the reflection of GOD's truth in a world of deception. Their task is not to conquer empires but to preserve memory, to shine in hidden places, to resist erasure by remembering.

The Remnant's Weapons

The remnant does not usually fight with swords or armies as their primary weapons, although they can and sometimes do. Their primary weapons are spiritual and informational:

- Scripture- the written memory of covenant.
- Testimony- the spoken remembrance of GOD's acts.
- Prayer- the invocation of divine presence against estrangement.
- Fellowship- the covenantal gathering that resists isolation.
- Education- They educate others, most times informally, in conversation, or through social media.

These primary weapons are simple yet unbreakable. They are the arsenal of remembrance, the tools by which light endures.

Historical Remnants

- The Essenes preserved scriptures in caves while empires burned libraries.
- The Waldensians carried the Word in hidden valleys during medieval persecution.
- The Underground Church in Soviet lands preserved faith under totalitarian control.
- Faithful families across ages quietly taught children, sang hymns, and remembered covenant when public worship was forbidden.

- The Knight Templars taught people to read the bible under risk of being put to death by the Church.

Each remnant was small, often despised, yet their light endured. Empires fell, but the remnant's memory survived.

Modern Remnants

Today, the remnant is scattered but present.
- Bloodline families still carry covenantal memory, though they are watched and manipulated by estranged powers.
- Secret fellowships continue their work, some known, some hidden, preserving archives and resisting councils.
- House churches and faithful communities gather in remembrance, resisting erasure.
- Truth-tellers and preservers expose deception and guard memory.

The remnant is not defined by numbers but by faithfulness. They are the quiet resistance, the hidden light, the preservers of covenant in an age of estrangement.

The Remnant's Commission

The remnant is not passive. They are commissioned to:
- Preserve memory when archives are erased.
- Guard bloodlines when corruption seeks to infiltrate.
- Bear witness when truth is silenced.
- Shine light when darkness prevails.
- Prepare the way for restoration when judgment falls.

Their task is not to overthrow empires but to endure them, to carry covenant through fire and flood, to ensure that memory is never extinguished.

Conclusion of Chapter 7

The remnant of light is the hope of history. While estrangement builds councils, machinery, and rituals of control, the remnant preserves covenant. Some are families whose bloodlines have carried light for millennia, even as the Watchers' minions attempt to watch and manipulate them. Some are secret fellowships, enduring across centuries, fighting in silence. Others are ordinary faithful, gathering in homes and hearts.

Empires fall, but the remnant endures. Councils conspire, but the remnant remembers. Darkness rises, but GOD's remnant shines. And in the end, it is the remnant of light (families, fellowships, and faithful) that carries history forward into restoration.

Chapter 8 -
Weapons of Remembrance

"This day shall be unto you for a memorial; and ye shall keep it a feast to the LORD throughout your generations; ye shall keep it a feast by an ordinance forever."
- Exodus 12:14

The remnant does not usually fight with armies or empires. Their primary arsenal is remembrance. Where estrangement from GOD thrives on erasure, HIS remnant resists by remembering. To recall covenant is to wage war against silence; to preserve memory is to strike at the heart of deception. The weapons of remembrance are not forged of steel but of testimony, scripture, fellowship, and covenantal practice. They are the arsenal of light in an age of darkness.

Memory as Warfare

The Watchers' strategy has always been erasure. Burn the scrolls, silence the prophets, fracture the timelines, confuse the language... and covenant is forgotten. But remembrance is the counter-weapon. To remember GOD's actions and words, to speak HIS name, to preserve HIS covenant, is to resist estrangement at its very root.

Every act of remembrance is an act of war against GOD's enemies. Every testimony spoken, every scripture read, every covenant meal shared is a strike against the enemy's machinery of control.

The Scriptural Foundation of Remembrance

Remembrance is not nostalgia. It is covenantal warfare, a weapon wielded against estrangement:
- Passover was instituted as a memorial, a weapon against forgetfulness (Exodus 12:14).
- The Psalms are songs of remembrance, rehearsing GOD's acts of deliverance.
- The Lord's Supper practiced by Christians is a covenantal act of remembrance: "This do in remembrance of Me" (Luke 22:19).
- The Sabbath itself is remembrance- a weekly act of resistance against the machinery of endless labor.

The Arsenal of the Remnant

The remnant's primary weapons are simple yet unbreakable:
- Scripture- the written memory of GOD's covenant, preserved against erasure.

- Testimony- the spoken remembrance of deliverance, carried across generations.
- Fellowship- the gathering of the faithful, resisting isolation and silence.
- Prayer- the invocation of GOD's presence, piercing the veil of estrangement.
- Fasting- a spiritual offering and physical discipline to help give clarity and bring one closer to GOD.
- Symbols and Rituals- bread, wine, oil, water... physical acts that anchor human memory.

These are not passive practices. They are spiritual weapons, sharpened by faith, wielded against the councils of estrangement.

Bloodlines and Remembrance

Across the millennia, certain families have served as vessels of covenantal memory... preserving scripture, testimony, and spiritual practice even under persecution. These bloodlines do not merely inherit faith; they inherit remembrance as warfare.

Examples include:
- The Kohanim (Jewish priestly lineage)- Descendants of Aaron, the Kohanim have preserved priestly duties and blessings for millennia, even in diaspora (dispersion of the Israelites around the world from Israel). Their rituals, such as the priestly blessing, and their oral traditions embody covenantal continuity. Even when scattered across continents, they maintained identity through liturgy and family practice, proving that remembrance can survive exile.

- The Griot families of West Africa- These hereditary oral historians preserve genealogies, songs, and spiritual wisdom across generations. Their memory resists colonial erasure and sustains communal identity. By carrying ancestral stories and sacred histories in song, they ensure that even when written records are destroyed, the covenant of memory endures.
- The Waldensians of Italy and France- This Christian remnant preserved scripture and testimony through centuries of persecution. Families often passed down faith in secret gatherings, teaching children hymns and scripture by candlelight. Their endurance in hidden valleys became a living testimony that remembrance can outlast empire.
- The Syriac Christian families of Mesopotamia- Preserving liturgy in the Syriac language, they carried covenantal witness through centuries of conquest and war. Their prayers, hymns, and manuscripts became anchors of remembrance, ensuring continuity even when surrounded by hostile powers.

These families often carry:
- Sacred heirlooms- scrolls, prayer books, relics, icons.
- Oral testimonies- miracles, martyrdoms, divine encounters.
- Ritual observances- Sabbath meals, covenantal prayers, anointing rites.

The Watchers target these and other remnant bloodlines. They sow division, trauma, and false doctrine to fracture generational memory. Yet the remnant within these families endures, becoming intergenerational sentinels who guard truth across time.

Even today, families teach covenantal memory in homes, resisting cultural indoctrination. Every story told, every prayer whispered, every tradition upheld is a strike against estrangement from GOD.

Secret Fellowships of Memory

Beyond families, hidden fellowships have preserved remembrance in silence. These are not merely religious orders. They are spiritual enclaves, commissioned to guard covenantal truth when empires burn libraries and rewrite chronicles.

Some examples include:

- The Essenes: A Jewish sect that preserved sacred texts in the Dead Sea Scrolls, hidden in caves to resist Roman destruction.
- Early Christian house churches: Operating under Roman persecution, these fellowships preserved apostolic teachings and practiced communion in secret.
- The Druze and Yazidi communities: Though not Christian, these Middle Eastern groups preserve spiritual memory through encrypted oral tradition and guarded rituals.

These fellowships often:
- Guard archives- scrolls, codices, encrypted digital texts.
- Practice symbolic rites- anointing, foot washing, covenant meals.
- Operate in silence- not out of fear, but strategic fidelity.

Their secrecy is tactical. Visibility invites infiltration. Their archives may never be published, their names never known. Yet their impact is eternal. They are the hidden backbone of remembrance.

Modern parallels include:
- Underground churches in authoritarian regimes, preserving scripture and testimony under surveillance.
- Encrypted digital fellowships, sharing truth across censored networks.
- Remnant communities, gathering in homes and forests to resist institutional apostasy.

These fellowships do not seek fame. They seek fidelity. Their arsenal is remembrance. Their battlefield is time. And their victory is endurance.

Mythic and Cultural Echoes

Cultures across the world preserve memory of remembrance as weapon:
- The Druids preserved oral traditions against Roman erasure.
- The Griots of Africa carried genealogies and histories through song.
- The Bards of Europe preserved memory in verse when literacy was rare.
- The Storytellers of Indigenous Nations carried covenantal memory through oral tradition.

Each culture remembers the same truth: remembrance is survival, and survival is resistance.

Modern Weapons of Remembrance

Today, the remnant wields remembrance in new forms:
- Digital archives that preserve truth against censorship.
- Independent fellowships that gather outside sanctioned institutions.
- Testimonies shared across networks, piercing propaganda.
- Families teaching children covenantal memory in homes.

Even in an age of surveillance and manipulation, remembrance endures. The remnant adapts, but the weapons remain the same.

The Remnant's Commission

The remnant is commissioned to wield remembrance as weapon:
- To speak truth when silence is demanded.
- To preserve scripture when archives are erased.
- To teach children when schools indoctrinate.
- To gather in covenant when councils forbid it.

Their primary arsenal is not of steel but of memory. Their battlefield is not only land but time. Their victory is not conquest but endurance.

Conclusion of Chapter 8

The weapons of remembrance are the remnant's arsenal. Scripture, testimony, fellowship, prayer, fasting, and covenantal practice are not passive traditions but active spiritual warfare. They resist erasure, preserve covenant, and strike at the heart of estrangement from GOD.

The Watchers and their councils fear remembrance, for it cannot be erased by fire, silenced by decree, or corrupted by pharmakeia. Families carry it in blood, fellowships preserve it in secret, and the faithful wield it in daily life.

Empires fall, but remembrance endures. Councils conspire, but remembrance resists. Darkness rises, but remembrance shines. For in the end, it is remembrance that preserves covenant, and covenant that secures victory in GOD.

Chapter 9 - Fracturing of Time

"And he shall speak great words against the most High, and shall wear out the saints of the most High, and think to change times and laws."
- Daniel 7:25

Time is covenantal. It is marked by GOD's appointed feasts, HIS Sabbaths, HIS seasons of remembrance. To fracture time is to fracture covenant, to sever humanity from memory and reorder reality itself. The Watchers and their councils have always sought to manipulate time... through calendars, through erasures, through distortions of memory. In our age, the fracturing of time has become one of the most subtle yet devastating weapons of estrangement from GOD.

Time as Covenant

From the beginning, GOD sanctified time. The seventh day was hallowed as Sabbath (Genesis 2:3). Israel was commanded to remember the feasts, each marking covenantal acts of deliverance. The Bible commanded mankind to follow the lunisolar calendar... a system that combining both lunar and solar elements, with the months are based upon the moon's phases and the years aligned to the solar year. This calendar is significant for determining the timing of required feasts and observances, to ensure holidays like Passover (Pesach) occur in the appropriate season.

The prophets warned against forgetting appointed times and feasts, for to forget them was to forget GOD's actions in our history. We must understand that time is not neutral. It is sacred. It is the rhythm of covenant. To fracture time is to help sever humanity from GOD's rhythm and bind them to estrangement from HIM.

The Watchers' Assault on Time

Daniel foresaw a ruler who would "think to change times and laws" (Daniel 7:25). This is the Watchers' strategy:
- Calendrical Corruption- shifting holy days, replacing GOD's feasts with pagan festivals.
- Historical Erasure- burning archives, rewriting chronicles, silencing testimonies.
- Chronological Confusion- fracturing genealogies, obscuring origins, severing continuity.

By altering time, estrangement severs memory. By severing memory, it severs covenant.

How We Got to the Current Gregorian Calendar

Rome and the Catholic church worked to replace the biblical lunisolar calendar:

- Julian Calendar- introduced under Julius Caesar in 46 BC, and based on a year length of 365.25 days, implemented by adding one leap day every four years, making the average Julian year exactly 365.25 days... slightly longer than the true tropical year, causing a slow drift of calendar dates over the centuries.
- Gregorian Calendar (used today by most of the world)- By the 16th century the drift in the Julian calendar had brought the spring equinox earlier in the calendar, affecting the calculation of Easter, so Pope Gregory XIII of the Catholic church adopted the Gregorian reform in 1582, which both removed a number of days to restore the equinox and changed the leap-year rule to reduce future drift.

Other Non-Biblical Calendars Used Today

Some other (possible lesser-known) non-biblical calendars are used in various parts of the world today:

- Islamic (Hijri) Calendar: Lunar-based, with 12 months totaling 354–355 days. Used for religious observances like Ramadan.
- Chinese Calendar: Lunisolar, guiding festivals like Lunar New Year.
- Hindu & Buddhist Calendars: Regional variations, often lunisolar, used for religious and cultural events.

- Other regional calendars: Examples include the Ethiopian calendar and the Persian (Solar Hijri) calendar, still official in countries like Ethiopia and Iran.

Ancient Examples of Fractured Time

Each empire sought not only to conquer land but to conquer time itself:
- Babylonian Captivity: Israel's calendar was disrupted, feasts forbidden, covenantal rhythms broken.
- Roman Calendar Reforms: Pagan festivals replaced GOD's appointed times, embedding estrangement in daily life.
- Medieval Erasures: Libraries burned, chronicles rewritten, timelines fractured to obscure covenantal memory.

Modern Fracturing of Time

Today, the fracturing of time has become systemic:
- Mandela Effect: Collective memory anomalies suggest manipulation of timelines, whether spiritual, technological, or psychological.
- Digital Erasure: Online archives vanish, histories are rewritten in real time, and yesterday's truth is today's "misinformation."
- Artificial Calendars: GOD's appointed times are ignored, replaced by secular holidays and consumer rituals.
- Acceleration of Time: Technology compresses experience, leaving humanity disoriented, unable to anchor memory.

The result is dislocation. Humanity drifts in fractured time, severed from covenantal rhythm, vulnerable to estrangement.

Bloodlines and Remembrance

While empires fracture time through calendars and erasures, certain families have carried covenantal rhythm across centuries. Their remembrance is not only spiritual but temporal. They preserve the appointed times of GOD, resisting assimilation into fractured calendars.

Examples of bloodlines preserving time include:
- Jewish families in diaspora- Even under Roman persecution, medieval exile, and modern pressures, Jewish families continued to mark Sabbaths and feasts according to the biblical lunisolar calendar. In ghettos and hidden communities, they lit Sabbath candles, recited prayers, and remembered covenantal rhythm, ensuring continuity even when empires sought to erase it.
- Coptic and Ethiopian Christians- These communities maintained their own calendars and feast cycles distinct from the Gregorian system. The Ethiopian calendar, still in use today, preserves rhythms tied to biblical tradition. Coptic families in Egypt continued to mark feasts such as Pascha and Epiphany according to their ancient reckoning, resisting assimilation into Western time systems.
- Indigenous nations- Many Native American and First Nations families preserved seasonal ceremonies tied to natural cycles. Harvest festivals, solstice rituals, and storytelling traditions resisted colonial imposition of Western time systems. These practices anchored identity

in covenantal rhythm with creation, even when colonial powers sought to impose artificial calendars.

- Armenian Christian families- Despite centuries of displacement and genocide, Armenian families preserved their liturgical calendar and feast cycles. Their remembrance of Easter, Vartanants (commemorating martyrdom), and other sacred times became acts of resistance against erasure.

These families act as custodians of time:
- Preserving genealogies that anchor covenantal continuity.
- Teaching children the rhythm of Sabbaths and feasts.
- Guarding oral traditions that resist chronological confusion.

The Watchers target these bloodlines by severing genealogies, distorting calendars, and erasing chronicles. Yet the remnant endures. Every family that remembers GOD's appointed times becomes a living resistance against fractured time.

Secret Fellowships and Timekeeping

Throughout history, remnant fellowships have acted as custodians of sacred time. Their mission was not only to preserve scripture but to safeguard the rhythm of covenant against imperial calendars and cultural erasure.

Some examples of timekeeping fellowships:
- The Qumran Community (Essenes): Preserved the Dead Sea Scrolls, which included calendrical texts detailing Sabbaths and feasts. Their strict observance of GOD's

appointed times resisted Roman and Hellenistic influence.

- Early Christian House Fellowships: In the Roman Empire, believers gathered secretly to celebrate the Lord's Supper and remember resurrection events according to sacred rhythms, even when imperial calendars imposed pagan festivals.
- Jewish Rabbinic Councils after the Temple's destruction: Preserved the lunisolar calendar and ensured continuity of feasts like Passover and Yom Kippur, despite exile and dispersion.
- Medieval Monastic Orders: Some monasteries quietly preserved chronicles and genealogies, anchoring sacred time when libraries were burned and histories rewritten.

Modern parallels:
- Underground churches in authoritarian regimes still mark Sabbaths and feasts in defiance of state calendars.
- Messianic fellowships today preserve the biblical lunisolar calendar, resisting assimilation into purely secular rhythms.
- Digital archivists and independent scholars act as custodians of time by preserving genealogical records and historical chronicles against digital erasure.

These fellowships understand that time is not neutral. Their secrecy is strategic: by hiding calendars, chronicles, and genealogies, they ensure covenantal rhythm survives even when empires fracture time.

Mythic and Cultural Echoes

Cultures across the world have preserved myths and traditions that echo the fracturing of time. These stories, though diverse, reveal a shared truth: time itself can be broken, reset, or manipulated.

Some examples include:
- Mayan Long Count Calendar: Spoke of great cycles and resets, suggesting epochs of destruction and renewal. These cycles echo covenantal warnings about forgetting appointed times.
- Hindu Yugas: Vast ages of decline and renewal, where dharma (cosmic order) erodes and must be restored. This mirrors biblical warnings about estrangement and restoration.
- Norse Ragnarok: A mythic end of time, where cosmic order collapses before a new age begins. It reflects the idea of fractured time leading to renewal.
- Indigenous Traditions: Many Native American nations speak of "time before time," when memory was broken and humanity had to relearn sacred rhythms through storytelling and ritual.
- Chinese Dynastic Cycles: The "Mandate of Heaven" concept tied cosmic order to rulers' fidelity. When rulers failed, time itself was seen as fractured, requiring renewal.

These echoes remind us that fractured time is not merely a biblical concern. It is a universal human experience. Across cultures, memory and rhythm are survival. To lose them is to lose identity; to preserve them is to resist estrangement from GOD.

The Remnant's Weapons Against Fractured Time

The remnant resists by remembering GOD's appointed times:

- Sabbath- weekly remembrance of creation and covenant.
- Feasts- annual memorials of deliverance and promise.
- Genealogies- preservation of lineage against erasure.
- Testimony- stories carried across generations, anchoring memory in time.

By keeping GOD's times, the remnant resists estrangement. By remembering, they heal fractured time.

Conclusion of Chapter 9

The fracturing of time is one of the Watchers' most insidious weapons. By altering calendars, erasing history, and distorting memory, they sever humanity from covenantal rhythm. Yet the remnant endures. Families preserve genealogies, fellowships guard calendars, and the faithful remember GOD's appointed times.

Empires fracture time, but the remnant restores it. Councils erase memory, but the remnant preserves it. Darkness disorients, but remembrance anchors. For in the end, time belongs not to estrangement but to GOD, who declares, "I AM the ALPHA and the OMEGA, the BEGINNING and the END" (Revelation 22:13).

Chapter 10 - Language of Confusion

"Come, let Us go down, and there confound their language, that they may not understand one another's speech."
- Genesis 11:7

Language is the vessel of memory. It carries covenant across generations, encodes testimony, and anchors identity. To fracture language is to fracture remembrance; to confuse speech is to help sever fellowship with GOD. From Babel to the present, estrangement has sought to weaponize words... twisting meaning, multiplying tongues, and corrupting communication. The war is not only over flesh and time, but over the very words by which truth is spoken.

Babel as Archetype

The Tower of Babel is the original model, the archetype, of linguistic estrangement. Humanity, united in one tongue, sought to build a tower to heaven. GOD descended, confounded their language, and scattered them across the earth (Genesis 11:1-9).

This was both judgment and mercy. Judgment, because rebellion to GOD was halted. Mercy, because estrangement from GOD was restrained. Yet the memory of Babel endures as a warning: language can be fractured, and when it is, covenantal unity is endangered.

Language as Weapon

The Watchers understood the power of words. Their teachings included enchantments, incantations, and manipulations of speech. Language became a tool of sorcery, a means of binding and deceiving.

In every age, estrangement has weaponized language:
- Redefinition- altering the meaning of words to obscure truth.
- Multiplication- creating jargon and dialects that divide rather than unite.
- Noise- flooding communication with distraction, drowning out remembrance.
- Silence- censoring speech, forbidding testimony, erasing words from memory.

Language is not neutral. It is another battlefield.

Ancient Echoes of Confusion

Each culture reveals the same pattern: language manipulated as a tool of estrangement:
- Egyptian Hieroglyphs: Priests controlled literacy, ensuring that only elites could interpret sacred texts.
- Babylonian Incantations: Words were used as spells, binding spirits and men alike.
- Greek Sophistry: Philosophers twisted words to win arguments rather than reveal truth.
- Roman Edicts: Laws were written to obscure, not clarify, binding populations in confusion.
- The old Roman Catholic Church: Made it heresy for non-clergy to be able to read the bible or its original languages... sometimes penalty for this was even death.

Modern Confusion of Language

Today, the confusion of language has reached new heights:
- Propaganda: Words are redefined daily, truth inverted, lies sanctified as "narrative."
- Political Correctness: Speech is policed, words forbidden, language reshaped to enforce compliance.
- Digital Noise: Endless streams of content drown out remembrance, leaving humanity disoriented.
- Artificial Tongues: Codes, algorithms, and machine languages mediate communication, severing direct human fellowship.

The result is Babel reborn... a world where words no longer unite but divide, where truth is obscured by confusion.

Bloodlines and Language

Certain families have carried language itself as a covenantal inheritance. Their preservation of words, dialects, and sacred names is not merely cultural - it is spiritual warfare against estrangement. These bloodlines resist assimilation by anchoring memory in speech, ensuring that covenantal cadence is not lost.

Examples of bloodlines preserving language include:

- Gaelic-speaking clans in Scotland and Ireland- For centuries, these clans preserved ancestral prayers, psalms, and oral traditions in Gaelic, even as English dominance sought to erase their tongue. Their songs and liturgies carried covenantal rhythm, resisting Anglicization and keeping alive the spiritual memory of their people.
- Basque families in Spain and France- Euskara, the Basque language, has no known relatives, making its survival extraordinary. Families preserved it through oral storytelling, folk songs, and secret gatherings, resisting repeated suppression by imperial powers. Their endurance demonstrates how language itself can be a covenantal inheritance, carried across centuries of pressure.
- Aramaic-speaking Assyrian Christian families in the Middle East- These families continue to use liturgical Aramaic, the language spoken by Christ and His apostles. Despite displacement and persecution, they preserved prayers, hymns, and scripture readings in Aramaic, carrying the cadence of ancient covenantal tongues into the present.

- Cherokee families in North America- Through Sequoyah's syllabary, Cherokee families preserved oral traditions, genealogies, and prayers in their own script. Even under forced assimilation and English-only policies, they resisted erasure by teaching children their language, ensuring continuity of covenantal identity.
- Māori families in New Zealand- Preserved prayers, chants, and genealogies in Te Reo Māori, resisting colonial suppression. Their oral traditions became anchors of identity, ensuring that covenantal rhythm survived even when pressured by Western systems.

These families act as linguistic guardians:
- Teaching children ancestral prayers and songs in native tongues
- Preserving genealogies and oral histories in original dialects
- Guarding sacred names and refusing to let them be erased or replaced

The Watchers target these bloodlines by suppressing minority languages, enforcing translations, and corrupting sacred words. Yet the remnant resists. Every word remembered in its original cadence is a strike against estrangement. Every name preserved is a testimony that covenant endures.

Secret Fellowships and the Word

Beyond families, hidden fellowships have preserved sacred language in silence. These groups understand that words are weapons, and that to guard them is to guard covenant itself. Their secrecy ensures survival when empires seek to erase tongues.

Examples of fellowships preserving the Word include:
- Kabbalistic circles in medieval Europe- Guarded Hebrew mystical texts, transmitting them in coded language to avoid persecution. Their symbolic speech and encrypted writings ensured that sacred words survived even under threat of death.
- Underground Bible translators in Reformation-era Europe- Risked their lives to render scripture into vernacular tongues, ensuring access to the Word for ordinary believers. Their clandestine work preserved covenantal truth against ecclesiastical censorship.
- Indigenous song-keeper societies in Oceania- Preserved chants, genealogies, and sacred names in native languages, resisting colonial erasure. Their oral liturgies became living archives of covenantal memory.
- Syriac monastic fellowships- Preserved liturgical Aramaic in manuscripts and chants, resisting assimilation into dominant tongues. Their monasteries became sanctuaries of language, ensuring continuity of sacred cadence.
- Byzantine hymnographers and monastic schools- Encoded theology in sacred poetry and hymnody, ensuring continuity of language and doctrine across centuries. Their chants preserved both rhythm and meaning, resisting cultural dilution.

Their practices include:
- Guarding archives- hidden manuscripts, coded texts, and oral liturgies

- Preserving cadence- chanting, singing, and reciting in sacred rhythm
- Protecting names- refusing to let divine titles be erased or replaced
- Encrypting language- using symbolic speech or coded ritual to preserve meaning under persecution

These fellowships are the custodians of the Word. They know that language is not neutral... it is covenantal. By preserving sacred tongues, they resist confusion. By guarding words, they resist silence. By proclaiming truth, they pierce the veil of estrangement.

Mythic and Cultural Echoes

Whether good or bad, cultures across the world preserve memory of their sacred language:
- The Vedas in India, preserved orally for millennia.
- The Qur'an recited in Arabic, resisting translation so as to preserve its cadence.
- The Torah read in Hebrew, anchoring covenant in the sacred tongue.
- Indigenous Songs and Chants carrying memory across generations.

Each culture remembers the same truth: language is sacred, and its preservation is resistance.

The Remnant's Weapons Against Confusion

The remnant resists linguistic estrangement by:
- Preserving Scripture in its original tongues.
- Teaching Children the words of covenant.

- Speaking Truth when silence is demanded.
- Guarding Names- especially the Name of GOD... against erasure.
- Fellowship in Word- gathering to read, sing, and proclaim truth.

These acts are not passive. They are warfare. Every word remembered is a strike against estrangement.

Conclusion of Chapter 10

The language of confusion is one of estrangement's most powerful weapons. By twisting words, multiplying tongues, and drowning truth in noise, the Watchers and their councils fracture covenantal unity. Yet the remnant endures. Families preserve sacred tongues, fellowships guard the WORD, and the faithful speak truth.

Empires confuse, but the remnant clarifies. Councils silence, but the remnant proclaims. Darkness obscures, but the remnant remembers. For in the end, it is not confusion that prevails, but the WORD of GOD, which endures forever (Isaiah 40:8).

Chapter 11 - Custodians of Silence

"Truth is fallen in the street, and equity cannot enter."
- *Isaiah 59:14*

Silence is not absence; it can also be strategy. The Watchers and their councils have always known that truth cannot be destroyed outright, but it can be buried, ridiculed, and silenced. Across history, custodians of silence have enforced a kind of amnesia... suppressing testimony, erasing archives, and punishing remembrance. To understand the war that continues today, one must see how silence itself has been weaponized.

Silence as Weapon

The machinery of control thrives not only on deception but on suppression. When truth threatens to surface, custodians of silence intervene. They ridicule witnesses, censor testimony, and erase records. Their goal is not to argue against truth but to bury it beneath noise and fear.

This silence of the righteous is ritualized. It is enforced by councils, legislated by empires, and sanctified by institutions. It is the counterfeit of covenantal remembrance... a liturgy of forgetting.

Ancient Custodians of Silence

Each age reveals the same pattern... truth suppressed, remembrance silenced, covenant buried:
- Egyptian Priesthoods: Restricted access to sacred texts, ensuring that only elites could interpret truth.
- Babylonian Scribes: Rewrote chronicles to glorify kings and erase covenantal memory.
- Roman Censors: Controlled speech, outlawed testimony, and silenced dissenters.
- Medieval Inquisitions: Burned manuscripts, executed witnesses, and enforced silence through terror.

Modern Custodians of Silence

Today, the custodians of silence wear new masks:
- Media Gatekeepers: Narratives are curated, dissenting voices erased.
- Academic Institutions: Research that challenges orthodoxy is ridiculed or suppressed.

- Digital Platforms: Algorithms bury truth, censor speech, and erase archives.
- Legal Systems: Whistleblowers are punished, testimonies sealed, records classified.

The methods have changed, but the strategy remains: silence truth, preserve estrangement from GOD.

Bloodlines Under Surveillance

The custodians of silence know that covenantal memory often flows through families. These bloodlines carry testimonies, genealogies, and rituals that resist erasure. Because of this, they are watched, monitored, and targeted. They are silenced not by argument but by suppression.

Examples of bloodlines under surveillance include:
- Huguenot families in France- During Catholic persecution, Huguenot families preserved Protestant testimony in secret. They met in caves, forests, and hidden homes, whispering prayers and passing down scripture orally. Their survival depended on silence, yet their faith endured across exile and diaspora, becoming a living witness against enforced forgetting.
- Crypto-Jewish families in Spain and Portugal (Conversos)- Under the Inquisition, many Jewish families outwardly converted to Christianity but secretly maintained fragments of Jewish ritual. They lit Sabbath candles in cupboards, whispered blessings, and passed down hidden traditions. Their silence was survival, but their memory was resistance, ensuring covenantal continuity even under threat of death.

- Armenian Christian families- After the genocide, Armenian families preserved testimony through oral histories, songs, and liturgical memory. Survivors told their stories in hushed tones, passing them to children and grandchildren. These testimonies became intergenerational archives, resisting attempts to erase their witness from history.
- Romani families in Europe- For centuries, Romani families preserved oral genealogies, songs, and traditions despite marginalization and forced assimilation. Their memory was carried in music and storytelling, resisting silence imposed by dominant cultures. Even when records were erased, their oral archives ensured continuity of identity.

These families endured by:
- Encoding testimony in ritual- lighting candles, singing hymns, or telling stories in private
- Preserving genealogies even when official records were erased
- Teaching children in silence- passing down memory in ways that evade surveillance

The Watchers and their councils monitor these families, attempting to fracture their continuity. Yet remembrance persists. Every hidden ritual, every whispered testimony, every preserved genealogy is a breach in the walls of silence.

Secret Fellowships and Hidden Archives

Alongside families, remnant fellowships have resisted silence by preserving truth in hidden archives. These fellowships understand that silence is not absence. It is strategy. Their secrecy ensures survival when public speech is forbidden.

Examples of fellowships preserving hidden archives include:

- The Lollards in England- Secretly copied and circulated vernacular scripture, resisting ecclesiastical bans. Their clandestine fellowships ensured that ordinary believers could access the Word, even when public reading was forbidden.
- Samizdat networks in the Soviet Union- Preserved banned books, testimonies, and chronicles by circulating truth in handwritten or typewritten form. These underground networks became lifelines of memory, resisting state censorship and enforced silence.
- Underground libraries in Nazi-occupied Europe- Preserved Jewish texts, testimonies, and cultural memory against systematic erasure. Hidden collections of manuscripts and oral archives ensured that covenantal identity survived even in ghettos and camps.
- Indigenous councils in the Americas- Preserved songs, genealogies, and sacred stories in hidden gatherings. Despite colonial suppression, these councils carried oral traditions across generations, ensuring that ancestral memory was not extinguished.

Their practices include:

- Hidden manuscripts- texts buried, concealed, or disguised to evade destruction
- Encrypted testimonies- truth preserved in coded language or symbolic ritual
- Silent gatherings- meetings held in secrecy, where memory was spoken aloud against enforced silence
- Oral archives- stories carried in memory when writing was forbidden

These fellowships are the custodians of remembrance in silence. They know that archives are not merely collections of words. They are weapons against estrangement. By preserving testimony in hidden places, they ensure that truth survives even when empires bury it.

Mythic and Cultural Echoes

Cultures across the world preserve memory of silence enforced:
- The Greek "Damnatio Memoriae"- erasing names from monuments to obliterate memory.
- The Chinese "Burning of Books" under Qin Shi Huang, silencing dissenting philosophies.
- The Soviet Erasures- photographs altered, names deleted, histories rewritten.
- Indigenous Oral Traditions- suppressed by colonizers, yet preserved in hidden songs and stories.

Each culture remembers the same truth: silence is not natural; it is enforced.

The Remnant's Response to Silence

The remnant resists silence by speaking:
- Testimony- telling stories even when forbidden.
- Scripture- reading aloud what empires forbid.
- Songs and Hymns- carrying truth in melody when words are censored.
- Fellowship- gathering in secret when public speech is silenced.

Every word spoken, every song sung, every testimony shared is a breach in the walls of silence.

Conclusion of Chapter 11

The custodians of silence are the enforcers of estrangement from GOD. They bury truth, ridicule witnesses, and erase memory. Yet the remnant endures. Families preserve testimony, fellowships guard archives, and the faithful speak truth even when forbidden.

Empires silence, but the remnant proclaims. Councils erase, but the remnant remembers. Darkness buries, but the remnant shines. For in the end, it is not silence that prevails, but the WORD of GOD, which cannot be bound (2 Timothy 2:9)

Chapter 12 - Hidden Preservers

"It is the glory of GOD to conceal a thing: but the honour of kings is to search out a matter."
- Proverbs 25:2

Not all custodians serve estrangement from GOD. While councils conspire in darkness and silence is enforced by fear, there have always been hidden preservers... men, women, families, and fellowships who guard memory in secret. They are the counter-custodians, the guardians of covenantal truth, the preservers of testimony. Some are known, others remain hidden, but their work has endured for millennia. To understand the endurance of covenant, one must see the hidden preservers who carry light through the shadows.

The Role of the Preserver

Where estrangement seeks to erase, the preserver safeguards. Where silence is enforced, the preserver whispers truth. Where archives are burned, the preserver hides scrolls. Their role is not conquest but endurance, not domination but preservation.

The hidden preservers are the reason covenantal memory has survived every empire. Without them, truth would have been extinguished. With them, it endures.

Biblical Archetypes of Preservation

- Joseph preserved grain in Egypt, ensuring survival through famine (Genesis 41).
- Ezra and the Scribes preserved the Law after exile, restoring covenantal memory.
- The Prophets preserved testimony even when kings sought to silence them.
- The Apostles preserved the words of Yeshuah (Jesus), carrying them across nations.

Each preserver acted in obscurity, yet their work shaped history.

Families as Hidden Preservers

Throughout history, certain families have carried preservation as their covenantal calling. They safeguarded genealogies, scriptures, and traditions across centuries, often unnoticed by the world but vital to the endurance of truth. Their preservation was not conquest but quiet endurance- a testimony to GOD's providence.

Examples of families as hidden preservers:
- Syriac Christian families in Mesopotamia- Preserved liturgical manuscripts in Syriac, ensuring continuity of worship even under imperial pressures. Their homes became sanctuaries of language and memory, where prayers and hymns were taught to children in secret, anchoring covenantal rhythm across generations.
- Coptic Christian families in Egypt- Carried fragments of ancient liturgy and scripture in Coptic, resisting assimilation into dominant languages. Their family traditions kept alive the cadence of ancient covenantal worship, ensuring that even when churches were pressured, the language of faith endured in households.
- Jewish scribal families in Yemen and across the diaspora- Preserved Torah scrolls and oral traditions in secrecy, maintaining covenantal continuity despite persecution. Fathers taught sons the art of copying scripture, ensuring accuracy and reverence. Their hidden manuscripts became lifelines of covenantal truth in times of exile.
- Armenian Christian families- After waves of persecution and genocide, Armenian families preserved testimony through oral histories, liturgical continuity, and family worship. Survivors told their stories in hushed tones, passing them to children and grandchildren. These testimonies became intergenerational archives, resisting attempts to erase their witness from history.

These families acted as custodians of memory by:
- Teaching children prayers, songs, and genealogies in ancestral tongues
- Hiding manuscripts and scrolls in homes or sacred spaces
- Encoding testimony in ritual and oral tradition when writing was forbidden

The Watchers and their councils sought to infiltrate and silence these families, but their endurance testifies that covenantal memory cannot be erased.

Secret Fellowships of Preservation

Alongside families, hidden fellowships have dedicated themselves to preservation. Their secrecy is not superstition but strategy... ensuring that archives, testimonies, and rituals survive when empires seek to erase them. These fellowships are the counter-custodians, guardians of covenantal truth.

Examples of fellowships as hidden preservers:
- Nestorian fellowships in Persia- Preserved manuscripts and liturgies in hidden monasteries, carrying covenantal memory eastward into Asia. Their archives became bridges of continuity, ensuring that scripture and worship survived across vast distances.
- Bogomil fellowships in the Balkans- Safeguarded scripture and testimony against both Catholic and Orthodox suppression. Their secrecy was survival, but their endurance ensured that covenantal witness was not extinguished.
- Underground Protestant fellowships in Japan (Kakure Kirishitan)- Preserved prayers and rituals in secrecy after Christianity was outlawed. Families and fellowships disguised prayers within local traditions, ensuring continuity of faith across centuries of suppression.
- Irish monastic networks during the Dark Ages- Preserved scripture and chronicles in remote monasteries, ensuring that biblical memory survived when much of Europe was

plunged into turmoil. Their illuminated manuscripts became anchors of covenantal remembrance.

- Samizdat fellowships in Soviet lands- Circulated banned Christian texts and testimonies in secrecy, ensuring that truth survived even under totalitarian control. Their hidden archives became lifelines of faith for believers under surveillance.

Their practices included:
- Hiding manuscripts in caves, monasteries, or disguised archives
- Carrying oral traditions in secret gatherings when writing was forbidden
- Encoding memory in symbols and rituals that concealed meaning from outsiders
- Preserving testimonies in silence until the time was right to speak

These fellowships testify that preservation is resistance. Their hidden archives and rituals ensured that covenantal memory survived every empire's attempt at erasure.

Mythic and Cultural Echoes

Cultures across the world preserve memory of hidden preservers:
- The Essenes at Qumran, hiding scrolls that would one day be discovered as the Dead Sea Scrolls.
- The Irish Monks who preserved scripture during the Dark Ages.
- The Griots of Africa who carried genealogies through song.
- Indigenous Elders who preserved stories in oral tradition despite colonization.

Each culture remembers the same truth: preservation is resistance, and resistance is remembrance.

Modern Hidden Preservers

Today, the preservers endure in new forms:
- Archivists and collectors safeguarding manuscripts and testimonies.
- Digital preservers creating backups of truth against censorship.
- Families teaching children covenantal memory in homes.
- Fellowships gathering in secret, preserving rituals and testimonies.

Even in an age of surveillance, preservation continues. The hidden preservers adapt, but their mission remains unchanged.

The Remnant's Commission to Preserve

The remnant is called not only to proclaim but to preserve:
- To guard scripture when archives are erased.
- To preserve testimony when silence is enforced.
- To protect bloodlines when corruption seeks to infiltrate.
- To safeguard memory when time is fractured.

Preservation is not passive. It is a type of warfare. Every archive hidden, every testimony remembered, every tradition carried is a strike against estrangement.

Conclusion of Chapter 12

The hidden preservers are the counter-custodians. While estrangement enforces silence, they preserve memory. While councils conspire, they safeguard covenant. While empires erase, they endure.

Some are families, carrying memory in blood. Some are fellowships, preserving archives in secret. Some are individuals, quietly teaching, writing, and remembering. Together, they ensure that covenant is never extinguished.

Empires erase, but the preservers endure. Councils silence, but the preservers whisper. Darkness buries, but the preservers guard the flame. For in the end, it is not silence that prevails, but remembrance... preserved by those hidden in GOD's providence.

Chapter 13 -
Covenant of the Table

"And thou shalt remember all the way which the LORD thy GOD led thee these forty years in the wilderness, to humble thee, and to prove thee, to know what was in thine heart."
- Deuteronomy 8:2

If estrangement from GOD thrives on erasure, then covenant with HIM thrives on remembrance. And nowhere is remembrance more embodied than at the table. From the Passover to GOD's prescribed feasts to hidden fellowships, the table has always been the place where covenant is renewed, memory is preserved, and light is shared. To understand how the remnant endures, one must see the covenant of the table... the meal that resists estrangement and anchors history in GOD's promises.

The Table as Covenant

From the beginning, meals have been covenantal:
- Abraham (Avram) prepared a feast for the three visitors at Mamre, sealing promise with hospitality (Genesis 18).
- Moses (Moshe) and the elders ate before GOD on Sinai after covenant was given (Exodus 24:9–11).
- Israel was commanded to keep the Passover meal as perpetual remembrance of deliverance (Exodus 12).
- The Christian New Testament instituted their Lord's Supper, commanding followers to remember through bread and wine (Luke 22:19–20).

The table is not merely nourishment. It is covenant enacted in flesh and blood, memory preserved in taste and ritual.

The Counterfeit Table

The Watchers and their councils have always sought to counterfeit the covenantal table.
- Pagan Feasts: Meals offered to idols, binding participants in estrangement.
- Banquets of Empire: Feasts that glorified kings and rulers rather than GOD.
- Modern Tables: Consumer rituals that replace covenant with indulgence, communion with consumption.

The counterfeit table feeds the body but starves the soul. It is ritual without remembrance, fellowship without covenant with GOD.

The Table as Resistance

For the remnant, the table is resistance:
- In Egypt, Israel ate the Passover in defiance of Pharaoh.
- In Babylon, Daniel and his companions resisted by refusing the king's food, choosing covenantal diet instead (Daniel 1).
- In Rome, the early church gathered in homes, breaking bread in remembrance, resisting the empire's banquets.

Every covenantal meal is an act of defiance. It declares that allegiance belongs not to man's empires but to GOD.

Bloodlines and the Table

Family bloodlines often preserve covenant through meals. The table becomes a living archive where memory is carried forward in taste, ritual, and fellowship. These meals are not just cultural. They are covenantal acts of remembrance.

Examples of bloodlines preserving the table:
- Jewish families across the diaspora- Preserved the Passover Seder, Sabbath meals, and feast cycles even under exile and persecution. Their tables became sanctuaries of covenantal memory, ensuring continuity of GOD's rhythm across centuries. Every blessing over bread and wine was a declaration that covenant endures despite empire.
- Armenian Christian families- Preserved liturgical feasts and commemorative meals tied to martyrdom and deliverance. Even after genocide, their tables carried testimony of survival and covenantal remembrance,

ensuring that children learned both faith and history through shared meals.

- Mennonite families- Preserved simple communal meals tied to humility and covenantal fellowship. Their tables resisted assimilation into indulgent feasts, embodying covenantal remembrance through simplicity and prayer.
- Coptic Christian households in Egypt- Maintained fasting and feasting cycles, anchoring family life in covenantal rhythm despite pressures to conform. Their tables became places of resistance, where covenantal prayers and blessings were preserved in secrecy when public worship was restricted.

These families act as custodians of the table by:
• Teaching children prayers and blessings at mealtime
• Preserving recipes and rituals that embody covenantal memory
• Gathering in defiance of estrangement, even when public worship is forbidden

The Watchers seek to corrupt these tables, turning them into indulgence or distraction. Yet the remnant resists. Every covenantal meal becomes a declaration that memory endures and covenant cannot be erased.

Secret Fellowships and Hidden Tables

Beyond families, remnant fellowships have gathered at hidden tables to preserve covenant in secrecy. These tables are altars of remembrance, where bread, wine, and fellowship anchor covenant against silence.

Examples of hidden fellowships preserving the table:

- Waldensian fellowships in the Alps- Gathered secretly to share covenantal meals, resisting persecution and preserving scripture in hidden valleys. Their tables became places of remembrance where bread and wine testified against empire.
- Underground Protestant fellowships in Reformation Europe - Shared bread and wine in secret gatherings, anchoring covenantal memory when public worship was forbidden. Their hidden tables carried the rhythm of GOD's covenant through centuries of suppression.
- House churches under Soviet rule- Gathered quietly to break bread and remember GOD's promises, resisting state suppression. Their tables became sanctuaries of fellowship, where testimony and scripture were preserved in silence.
- Quaker meetings in England and America- Preserved communal meals and testimonies in hidden gatherings, anchoring covenantal memory in simplicity and fellowship. Their tables embodied resistance to estrangement by centering on GOD's presence rather than empire's demands.

Their practices included:
- Hidden communion disguised as ordinary meals
- Silent testimonies spoken at the table when pulpits were silenced
- Encoded rituals where food and drink carried covenantal meaning
- Preserved oral archives where recipes and prayers were carried in memory

These fellowships testify that the covenantal table cannot be erased. Even when empires ban remembrance, the remnant gathers in hidden places, breaking bread as resistance and declaring covenant in silence.

Mythic and Cultural Echoes

Cultures across the world preserve memory of sacred meals:
- Greek Symposia- feasts where philosophy and ritual mingled.
- Norse Blots- sacrificial feasts binding clans in covenant.
- Indigenous Feasts- meals shared in remembrance of ancestors and spirits.
- Christian Eucharist- the covenantal meal that has endured for two millennia.

Each culture remembers the same truth: meals are not only nourishment, they are covenant with GOD.

The Remnant's Commission at the Table

The remnant is called to preserve the covenant of the table:
- To gather in remembrance when estrangement demands silence.
- To teach children covenantal memory through meals.
- To resist counterfeit feasts that glorify empire rather than GOD.
- To preserve fellowship when isolation is enforced.

The table is not only nourishment but a type of warfare. Every covenantal meal is a strike against estrangement to GOD.

Conclusion of Chapter 13

The covenant of the table is one of the remnant's anchors. While estrangement from GOD builds counterfeit feasts, HIS remnant gathers in remembrance. While councils conspire in darkness, the remnant breaks bread in light. While empires demand allegiance, the remnant declares covenant at the table.

Empires feast, but the remnant remembers. Councils banquet, but the remnant communes. Darkness consumes, but the remnant shines. For in the end, it is the covenant of the table (the remembrance of GOD's deliverance) that endures forever.

Part III -
Convergence and Confrontation

Chapter 14 - Engines of Deception

"Woe unto them that call evil good, and good evil; that put darkness for light, and light for darkness."
- Isaiah 5:20

If remembrance is one of the weapons of GOD's remnant, deception is one of the weapons of estrangement from HIM. The Watchers and their councils have always thrived on lies. Not simple falsehoods, but engineered systems of deception. These are engines, vast and intricate, designed to distort perception, fracture memory, and enslave nations. To understand the war that continues, one must see how deception has been mechanized into engines that drive history itself.

Deception as System

Deception is not merely a lie told; it is a system that is built. The Watchers have institutionalized deception, embedding it in religion, politics, economy, and culture. Their engines of deception are not accidents but deliberate constructs, designed to obscure truth and enthrone estrangement from GOD.

Ancient Engines of Deception

Almost every empire has built engines of deception... systems that disguised estrangement as enlightenment:
- Egyptian Priesthoods: Cloaked idolatry in ritual, presenting bondage as divine order.
- Babylonian Astrology: Replaced covenantal time with celestial manipulation, binding nations to stars rather than GOD.
- Greek Philosophy: Twisted wisdom into sophistry, elevating human reason above divine revelation.
- Roman Propaganda: Declared emperors divine, sanctifying tyranny as salvation.

Modern Engines of Deception

Today, the engines are more sophisticated, but the pattern remains:
- Media Empires: Narratives curated, truth inverted, lies repeated until believed.
- Educational Systems: History rewritten, memory fractured, covenant erased.
- Scientific Dogmas: Theories exalted as unquestionable truth, dissent silenced.

- Digital Platforms: Algorithms manipulate perception, shaping reality itself.
- Political Machinery: Promises of freedom masking systems of control.

These are not just about isolated lies of commission or omission, but engines… vast systems designed to perpetuate deception.

Bloodlines Targeted by Deception

The engines of deception do not merely distort nations; they target families who preserve covenantal memory. These bloodlines carry testimonies, genealogies, and rituals that resist estrangement. Because of this, they are prime targets for ridicule, distortion, and suppression.

Examples of bloodlines targeted by deception:
- Huguenot families in exile- Mocked as heretics and slandered by propaganda, yet they preserved covenantal worship across generations. Their hidden gatherings and whispered prayers carried testimony of GOD's deliverance even when empire sought to erase them.
- Crypto-Jewish families in Spain and Portugal (Conversos)- Forced to conceal their identity under the Inquisition, their genealogies were obscured by deception. Yet they preserved fragments of Sabbath observance and blessings in secrecy, ensuring that covenantal memory survived beneath layers of distortion.
- Armenian Christian families- After waves of persecution and genocide, Armenian families preserved testimony through oral histories and liturgical meals. Deception sought to erase their witness, but their tables and prayers carried covenantal remembrance forward.

- Eastern European Jewish families- Targeted by propaganda that caricatured and slandered them, their traditions were ridiculed as superstition. Yet they preserved Torah study, Sabbath meals, and genealogies in secrecy, ensuring continuity of covenantal truth.

These families endured by:
- Preserving testimony in oral tradition when written records were erased
- Teaching children covenantal prayers and songs in secrecy
- Encoding genealogies in ritual and symbol when deception obscured history

The Watchers and their councils sought to drown these families in distortion, but their endurance testifies that truth cannot be erased by deception.

Secret Fellowships Against Deception

Alongside families, remnant fellowships have resisted the engines of deception. These fellowships understand that deception is systemic, and their mission is to expose lies, preserve truth, and guard memory against distortion.

Examples of fellowships resisting deception:
- The Lollards in England- Resisted ecclesiastical deception by secretly translating and sharing scripture. Their hidden fellowships exposed lies through testimony and preserved GOD's Word against distortion.
- Underground Protestant fellowships in France- Gathered in forests and caves to proclaim truth against state

deception. Their hidden tables and prayers dismantled propaganda by anchoring memory in covenant.
- Waldensian fellowships in the Alps- Preserved scripture and testimony in secrecy, resisting persecution and exposing deception by living covenantal truth.
- Samizdat fellowships in Soviet lands- Circulated banned Christian texts and testimonies, dismantling propaganda by preserving truth in hidden archives. Their clandestine networks ensured that GOD's Word endured even under totalitarian deception.

Their practices included:
- Preserving hidden archives of scripture and testimony
- Guarding oral traditions in secret gatherings
- Exposing lies through lived testimony and witness
- Encoding truth in ritual and symbol when words were forbidden

These fellowships testify that deception can be resisted. Their archives, testimonies, and rituals dismantle engines of distortion, exposing lies and preserving covenantal truth.

Mythic and Cultural Echoes

Cultures across the world preserve memory of deception as system:
- Plato's Cave- shadows mistaken for reality.
- Maya Illusion in Hindu thought- the world as deception, truth hidden beneath.
- Trickster Figures in folklore- deceivers who manipulate perception.
- Prophetic Warnings- Isaiah, Jeremiah, and others denouncing false prophets and lying priests.

Each culture remembers the same truth: deception is not random but systemic.

Some of the Remnant's Weapons Against Deception

The remnant resists deception with truth:
- Scripture- the unchanging Word of GOD.
- Discernment- the Spirit's gift to see through lies.
- Testimony- lived truth that counters propaganda.
- Fellowship- communities that preserve memory against distortion.
- Remembrance- anchoring in covenant when deception seeks to erase.

These weapons dismantle deception's engines, exposing lies and bringing them into the light.

Conclusion of Chapter 14

The engines of deception are the Watchers' most enduring constructs. From ancient temples to modern media, from Babylonian astrology to digital algorithms, the pattern remains: lies institutionalized, deception mechanized, estrangement enthroned.

Yet the remnant endures. Families preserve truth, fellowships resist distortion, and the faithful wield remembrance as weapon. Empires deceive, but the remnant discerns. Councils lie, but the remnant proclaims. Darkness manipulates, but the remnant shines. For in the end, it is not deception that prevails, but the truth of GOD which cannot be broken.

Chapter 15 - Mandela of Memory

"And he shall speak great words against the most High, and shall wear out the saints of the most High, and think to change times and laws."
- Daniel 7:25

Memory is covenantal. It is the thread that ties generations together, the anchor of identity, the vessel of testimony. To fracture memory is to fracture covenant itself. In recent years, strange anomalies have surfaced... collective memories that differ from recorded history, details remembered by millions yet denied by archives. This phenomenon, popularly called the Mandela Effect, is more than mere curiosity. It is a sign of the war over memory, a glimpse into the manipulation of perception, and a warning that estrangement has extended its engines into the very fabric of remembrance.

Memory as Covenant

Throughout Scripture, GOD commands His people to remember:
- "Remember the Sabbath day, to keep it holy" (Exodus 20:8).
- "Thou shalt remember all the way which the LORD thy GOD led thee" (Deuteronomy 8:2).
- "This do in remembrance of Me" (Luke 22:19).

Memory is not optional; it is covenantal. To remember is to remain in covenant with GOD. To forget is to drift into estrangement.

The Assault on Memory

The Watchers and their councils have always sought to corrupt memory:
- Erasure: Burning archives, silencing testimonies, rewriting chronicles.
- Confusion: Multiplying narratives, distorting language, fracturing timelines.
- Replacement: Substituting false memories, embedding propaganda, enforcing new "truths."

The Mandela Effect may be the latest manifestation of this ancient war... a sign that memory itself is being manipulated on a global scale.

The Mandela Effect: A Modern Sign

The term arose when many remembered Nelson Mandela dying in prison in the 1980s, though official history records his release and later presidency. Since then, countless anomalies have been reported:

- Logos and brand names remembered differently.
- Famous lines in films quoted one way by millions, yet recorded another.
- Historical details recalled by groups yet denied by archives.

These anomalies are often dismissed as faulty memory. But the scale, consistency, and persistence suggest something deeper: a fracturing of memory itself.

Possible Explanations

The Mandela Effect has been interpreted in many ways:

- Psychological: Collective false memory, the brain filling gaps with familiar patterns.
- Spiritual: Manipulation of memory by estranged powers, sowing confusion.
- Technological: Experiments in quantum physics, AI, or digital archives altering perception.
- Temporal: Shifts in timelines, parallel realities bleeding into one another.

Whatever the mechanism, the effect is the same: memory is destabilized, covenant is threatened, and humanity is left disoriented.

Bloodlines and Memory

Memory is covenantal, and certain families have carried remembrance as their inheritance. These bloodlines preserve genealogies, testimonies, and rituals across generations, resisting manipulation even when archives are erased or distorted. Because of this, they are prime targets for deception and ridicule.

Examples of bloodlines preserving memory:
- Assyrian Christian families- Preserved prayers and oral testimonies in Aramaic, carrying memory across centuries despite persecution and displacement. Their homes became sanctuaries of remembrance, where children learned hymns and prayers that anchored covenantal identity.
- Samaritan families- Maintained genealogical continuity and Torah traditions in secrecy, resisting assimilation into dominant cultures. Their preservation of the Samaritan Pentateuch and ritual practices ensured that covenantal memory endured even when pressured by surrounding powers.
- Jewish families across Eastern Europe- Preserved Sabbath observance, Torah study, and oral testimonies even under pogroms and later under Nazi persecution. Their genealogies and rituals became lifelines of covenantal memory when archives were destroyed.
- Polish Catholic families under communism- Preserved testimonies of faith and resistance in oral stories, resisting state propaganda that sought to erase covenantal memory. Their prayers, hymns, and hidden gatherings carried remembrance forward when public worship was restricted.

These families endure by:
- Teaching children ancestral prayers and testimonies in native tongues
- Preserving genealogies orally when written records are destroyed

- Encoding memory in ritual and symbol when deception obscures history

The Watchers and their councils sought to fracture these bloodlines through ridicule and distortion, but their endurance testifies that covenantal memory cannot be erased.

Secret Fellowships as Guardians of Memory

Alongside families, remnant fellowships have acted as guardians of memory. These fellowships understand that remembrance is warfare, and their mission is to preserve testimony against distortion. Their secrecy ensures survival when empires manipulate perception and fracture timelines.

Examples of fellowships preserving memory:
- The Cathars in medieval France- Preserved alternative testimonies and archives in secrecy, resisting ecclesiastical suppression. Their hidden fellowships carried memory forward even when empire sought to erase them.
- Underground Jewish fellowships during the Holocaust- Preserved oral testimonies, prayers, and hidden archives in ghettos and camps. Their clandestine gatherings ensured that covenantal memory endured even under systematic erasure.
- Waldensian fellowships in the Alps- Preserved scripture and testimony in hidden valleys, resisting persecution and distortion. Their secret gatherings became living archives of covenantal truth.
- Underground Christian fellowships in Soviet states- Preserved testimonies and scripture in hidden gatherings, resisting propaganda and distortion. Their fellowships

carried memory forward when official archives were censored or destroyed.

Their practices included:
- Hidden archives- scrolls, manuscripts, and testimonies concealed from destruction
- Oral traditions- stories carried in memory when writing was forbidden
- Encoded rituals- symbols and practices that preserved meaning beneath deception
- Silent testimonies- truth whispered in secrecy when public speech was silenced

These fellowships testify that fractured memory can be resisted. Their archives, testimonies, and rituals anchor covenantal remembrance against manipulation.

Mythic and Cultural Echoes

Cultures across the world preserve memory of fractured remembrance:
- Greek Lethe- the river of forgetfulness in Hades, where souls lost memory.
- Hindu Maya- illusion that veils true reality.
- Norse Yggdrasil- the tree of memory threatened by forces of chaos.
- Indigenous Traditions- stories of "time before time," when memory was broken.

Each culture remembers the same truth: memory can be fractured, and when it is, covenant is endangered.

The Remnant's Weapons Against Fractured Memory

The remnant resists the Mandela of memory by anchoring in GOD's truth:

- Scripture- the unchanging Word of GOD, preserved against distortion.
- Testimony- stories carried across generations, resisting erasure.
- Symbols and Rituals- covenantal acts that anchor memory in body and spirit.
- Fellowship- communities that preserve memory when individuals falter.
- Discernment- the Spirit's gift to see through deception and hold fast to truth.

These weapons ensure that even when memory is fractured, covenant endures.

Conclusion of Chapter 15

The Mandela Effect is more than curiosity. It is a sign of the war over memory, a glimpse into the manipulation of perception, and a warning that estrangement has extended its engines into remembrance itself. Yet the remnant endures. Families preserve testimony, fellowships guard archives, and the faithful anchor themselves in GOD's Word.

Empires fracture memory, but the remnant remembers. Councils manipulate perception, but the remnant discerns. Darkness confuses, but the remnant shines. For in the end, it is not fractured memory that prevails, but the eternal remembrance of GOD, who declares, "I am the LORD, I change not" (Malachi 3:6).

Chapter 16 -
Council Beneath the Earth

"They search out iniquities; they accomplish a diligent search: both the inward thought of every one of them, and the heart, is deep."
- Psalm 64:6

Not all councils convene in palaces or temples. Some gather in hidden places... beneath mountains, in caverns, in subterranean halls where secrecy is absolute. From the Watchers' descent on Hermon to the whispers of underground assemblies in every age, there has always been memory of councils beneath the earth. These are not merely legends of caves and tunnels, but testimonies of hidden governance, where estranged powers and their human agents conspire beyond the sight of nations. To understand the machinery of estrangement, one must descend into the depths, where the council beneath the earth plots in shadow.

The Depths as Domain

Scripture often associates the depths with estrangement.
- The Abyss: Revelation 9 speaks of the bottomless pit, from which locust-like beings emerge.
- The Rephaim: Isaiah 14 describes the shades of the underworld rising to greet fallen kings.
- The Watchers' Binding: 1 Enoch records that the rebellious angels were bound in subterranean prisons until judgment.

The depths are not neutral. They are the domain of estrangement, the hidden chambers where rebellion festers.

Ancient Memories of Subterranean Councils

- Mesopotamian Myths: The Apkallu, semi-divine sages, were said to dwell beneath the waters and emerge to instruct kings.
- Greek Hades: The underworld was ruled by councils of gods and judges, determining the fate of souls.
- Mesoamerican Lore: The Popol Vuh describes Xibalba, the underworld ruled by lords who tested and deceived humanity.
- Celtic Traditions: Tales of hollow hills and subterranean courts of the Sidhe, who manipulated human affairs from beneath the earth.

Each culture remembers the same truth: councils beneath the earth, hidden rulers shaping destiny from the shadows.

The Watchers' Legacy Underground

The oath on Hermon did not end on the mountain. Many traditions suggest that the Watchers, once bound, continued to influence humanity from subterranean prisons. Their knowledge was preserved in hidden councils, passed through bloodlines and secret fellowships.

These councils beneath the earth became the prototypes of other nefarious clandestine secret societies, hidden orders, and shadow governments. Their secrecy is not incidental but essential... for estrangement thrives in darkness.

Modern Testimonies of Subterranean Councils

In the modern age, whispers persist of underground assemblies:
- Military Bunkers and Deep Facilities: Places where decisions are made beyond public oversight.
- Secret Networks: Alleged councils meeting in hidden chambers, blending politics, finance, and occult ritual.
- Subterranean Myths: Stories of tunnels beneath cities, caverns beneath mountains, and hidden halls where rulers conspire.

Whether literal or symbolic, these testimonies echo the same pattern: councils beneath the earth, hidden from sight, shaping the world above.

Bloodlines Watched from Below

Throughout history, certain families have carried covenantal memory like a living archive. These bloodlines are vessels of continuity, bearing witness across centuries. Because they preserve identity and resist assimilation, they draw the gaze of subterranean councils that seek to fracture their inheritance.

Examples of bloodlines watched from below:
- Hebrew priestly families (Kohanim and Levites)- Preserved genealogical records and priestly blessings across exile and dispersion. Even when temples were destroyed, their lineage carried covenantal continuity, resisting erasure.
- Greek Orthodox Christian families under Ottoman rule- Maintained liturgical traditions and family worship in secrecy, resisting forced conversion and preserving covenantal rhythm through hidden prayers.
- Jewish families in Prague and Central Europe- Safeguarded Torah scrolls and rabbinic writings in hidden archives during waves of persecution, ensuring covenantal testimony survived beneath empire's watchful eye.
- Catholic recusant families in England- Preserved faith in secrecy during centuries of suppression, gathering in hidden chapels and passing down prayers and testimonies within households.

These families endured by:
- Teaching children prayers and blessings in secrecy
- Preserving genealogies orally when records were destroyed
- Encoding covenantal testimony in ritual and symbol when deception obscured history

Their resilience testifies that covenantal memory can outlast subterranean schemes, carrying light through generations even when shadowed by unseen watchers.

Secret Fellowships in Opposition

Against councils of darkness, hidden fellowships arose - not conspiracies of power, but sanctuaries of preservation. These fellowships formed networks of resistance that outlasted empires, ensuring that covenantal truth endured.

Examples of secret fellowships in opposition:
- Early Christian catacomb fellowships in Rome- Gathered beneath the city to break bread, preserve scripture, and resist imperial suppression. Their hidden tables became altars of remembrance in the depths.
- Jesuit underground fellowships in Reformation-era Europe- Preserved scripture, education, and testimony in secrecy, resisting persecution and ensuring continuity of covenantal teaching.
- Hidden Jewish yeshivot (schools) in Eastern Europe- Preserved Torah study and oral tradition in clandestine schools, resisting state and ecclesiastical suppression. Their fellowships carried covenantal truth across generations.
- Scottish Covenanter fellowships- Gathered in secret fields and caves to preserve worship and testimony when public assemblies were forbidden. Their hidden gatherings became living archives of resistance.

Their practices included:
- Concealing scripture in caves, catacombs, or disguised archives
- Preserving oral traditions in secret gatherings when writing was forbidden

- Encoding memory in ritual and symbol to protect meaning from outsiders
- Bearing silent testimony until the time was right to speak

These fellowships are the counter-councils: small circles of remembrance that resist subterranean estrangement, ensuring that even in the deepest shadows, the remnant's testimony endures.

Mythic and Cultural Echoes of Resistance

Each culture remembers not only councils of darkness but councils of light... hidden preservers resisting estrangement from GOD.

- The Maccabees: Preserved covenant in caves, resisting Antiochus' decrees.
- Early Christians: Gathered in catacombs beneath Rome, breaking bread in defiance of empire.
- Hidden Monks: Preserved scripture in mountain monasteries during invasions.
- Indigenous Resistance: Tribes hiding in caves and forests, preserving traditions against colonizers.

The Remnant's Commission Against Subterranean Councils

The remnant is called to resist councils beneath the earth by:
- Exposing deception when truth is buried.
- Preserving memory when archives are hidden.
- Gathering in covenant when secrecy is enforced.
- Anchoring in GOD's Word when councils conspire in darkness.

The remnant's strength is not in secrecy but in light. Their task is to shine even when councils plot beneath the earth.

Conclusion of Chapter 16

The council beneath the earth is the archetype of hidden estrangement. From ancient myths to modern testimonies, the pattern remains: rulers conspiring in darkness, estranged powers influencing from below, secrecy enthroned as governance.

Yet the remnant endures. Families preserve covenant, fellowships resist in secret, and the faithful anchor themselves in GOD's Word. Empires conspire beneath the earth, but the remnant shines above it. Councils plot in darkness, but the remnant remembers in light. For in the end, it is not the council beneath the earth that prevails, but the council of GOD, whose throne is established forever in heaven.

Chapter 17 -
Engines of War in Heaven and Earth

"And there was war in heaven: Michael and his angels fought against the dragon; and the dragon fought and his angels, and prevailed not."
- Revelation 12:7-8

War is not confined to the battlefield of men. It is cosmic, stretching from heaven's courts to earth's plains, from angelic hosts to human armies. The Watchers, once bound, left behind legacies of violence, technologies of destruction, and councils of war. Their engines of conflict echo in every age... from the swords of antiquity to the machines of modernity. To understand the fullness of estrangement, one must see how war is waged both in heaven and on earth, and how the remnant stands within this cosmic struggle.

War in Heaven

The book of Revelation unveils the original conflict: war in heaven itself. Michael and his angels fought against the dragon and his angels, and the dragon was cast down (Revelation 12:7–9). This was not metaphor but reality... a cosmic conflict that reverberated into creation.

The Watchers' rebellion was part of this war. Their descent to Mount Hermon was not isolated but connected to the larger conflict between GOD's hosts and estranged powers. Their oath, their corruption of flesh, their teaching of forbidden arts... all were engines of war against heaven's order.

Engines of War on Earth

The Watchers taught men the art of war: metallurgy, enchantments, and weaponry (1 Enoch 8:1). These teachings became engines of war on earth.

- Bronze and Iron: Forged into swords, spears, and chariots.
- Siege craft: Towers, walls, and engines of destruction.
- Alchemy and Sorcery: Substances and rituals used to empower armies.
- Idolatrous Warfare: Battles fought as sacrifices to gods, sanctifying bloodshed.

Every empire has built engines of war, not only to conquer land but to enthrone estrangement.

Ancient Echoes of Heavenly War

Cultures preserved memory of cosmic conflict:
- Mesopotamian Myths: Marduk battling Tiamat, order against chaos.
- Greek Titanomachy: Olympians warring against Titans, heaven against earthbound powers.
- Norse Ragnarök: The final battle between gods and giants, heaven and earth consumed in fire.
- Hindu Devas vs. Asuras: Celestial beings locked in endless war.

Each myth echoes the same truth: war is not only human but cosmic, engines of heaven and earth intertwined.

Modern Engines of War

Today, the engines of war have become global and technological:
- Industrial Warfare: Tanks, planes, and artillery... mechanized destruction.
- Nuclear Weapons: Fire that echoes apocalyptic prophecy, threatening creation itself.
- Cyber Warfare: Invisible battles fought in data and code, shaping nations without armies.
- Biological and Genetic Warfare: Manipulation of flesh itself, echoing the Watchers' corruption.

These are not merely human inventions. They are continuations of forbidden knowledge, engines of war seeded by estrangement from GOD and his true plan for humanity.

Bloodlines in the Crossfire

Family bloodlines that preserve covenantal memory are often caught in the crossfire of war. Empires conscript them, councils silence them, and estranged powers corrupt them. Yet these families endure, resisting engines of war by anchoring themselves in GOD's covenant.

Examples of endurance include:
- Jewish families of Vilna (Lithuania)- Preserved Torah study and oral testimony during waves of invasion and war. Even as ghettos and archives were destroyed, families carried covenantal prayers and genealogies in secrecy, ensuring continuity of remembrance.
- Syriac Orthodox families in Tur Abdin (Turkey)- Endured centuries of conflict and displacement, yet preserved liturgical memory in Aramaic. Their homes and monasteries became sanctuaries of covenantal witness amid violence.
- Bohemian Brethren families in Central Europe- Preserved worship and scripture in hidden communities during religious wars. Their family networks carried covenantal identity across generations despite suppression.
- Christian families in Armenia during Ottoman campaigns- Preserved testimonies of faith through oral tradition and hidden liturgy, resisting attempts to erase covenantal identity in times of war.

These families show that covenantal memory is not easily erased. Even when war seeks to conscript, silence, or destroy, bloodlines endure by carrying testimony across exile, persecution, and suppression.

Secret Fellowships of Resistance

Remnant fellowships have long resisted engines of war. Some preserved peace in hidden communities, refusing to serve empires. Others acted as guardians, protecting archives and bloodlines during times of conflict.

Examples include:
- The Hutterite fellowships in Moravia and later North America- Preserved communal worship and pacifist witness, resisting militarism by building agricultural fellowships centered on covenantal life. Their hidden endurance became testimony against engines of war.
- The Czech Brethren (Unitas Fratrum)- Formed clandestine circles to preserve scripture and worship during waves of suppression in Central Europe. Their fellowships carried covenantal truth forward when war sought to extinguish it.
- Hidden Jewish study circles in Kraków during World War II- Preserved Torah study and oral testimony in secrecy, resisting engines of war that sought to erase covenantal identity. Their clandestine gatherings became living archives of faith.
- Christian Anabaptist fellowships in Switzerland- Resisted conscription and persecution by gathering in forests and caves. Their secrecy preserved covenantal worship and testimony when war and empire demanded conformity.

These fellowships resisted not with armies but with memory, worship, and covenantal endurance. Their secrecy was not ambition but necessity. It was a way to preserve light when war sought to extinguish it.

The Remnant's Weapons in Cosmic War

The remnant does not fight with earthly engines but with spiritual weapons:

- Prayer- invoking GOD's power against estrangement.
- Scripture- the sword of the Spirit, sharper than any two-edged blade (Hebrews 4:12).
- Faith- the shield that quenches fiery darts (Ephesians 6:16).
- Testimony- overcoming by the blood of the Lamb and the word of their witness (Revelation 12:11).
- Remembrance- anchoring in covenant when deception and violence rage.

These weapons dismantle the engines of war, resisting estrangement with light.

The Final War

Scripture promises a final conflict:
- Armageddon: Nations gathered against GOD, only to be overthrown by His Word (Revelation 16:16).
- The Rider on the White Horse: leading heaven's armies (Revelation 19:11–16).
- The Binding of Satan: The dragon cast into the abyss, engines of war silenced forever (Revelation 20:1–3).

The engines of war will not endure. They will be dismantled by the one true GOD, who reigns forever.

Conclusion of Chapter 17

The engines of war span heaven and earth. From the Watchers' rebellion to modern arsenals, from cosmic battles to earthly conflicts, the pattern remains: estrangement thrives on violence, sanctifying bloodshed as necessity. Yet the remnant endures.

Families preserve covenant, fellowships resist war's machinery, and the faithful wield spiritual weapons.

Empires build engines of war, but the remnant builds altars of remembrance. Councils conspire in violence, but the remnant proclaims peace. Darkness wages war, but the remnant shines. For in the end, it is not engines of war that prevail, but the eternal reign of GOD, whose kingdom is peace everlasting.

Chapter 18 - The Grey Interlude

"The Nephilim were on the earth in those days, and also afterward, when the sons of GOD came in to the daughters of men, and they bore children to them. These were the mighty men who were of old, men of renown."
- Genesis 6:4

The Greys are not extraterrestrials. They are not saviors from the stars, nor explorers from distant galaxies. They are vessels... cloned bodies, engineered through forbidden sciences first revealed by the Watchers. When the Nephilim, the hybrid offspring of angels and women, were destroyed in the Flood, their souls were left without bodies. These disembodied spirits became what most traditions call "demons." But estrangement did not leave them wandering forever. Through genetic manipulation, the fallen angels created cloned vessels (the Greys) so that their children might once again inhabit flesh. The Grey interlude is not about alien visitation, but about the continuation of the Nephilim agenda through cloned bodies and demonic possession.

The Problem of the Nephilim Spirits

When the Nephilim perished in the Flood, their hybrid souls had no place to go. They were not fully human, and thus not eligible for redemption. They were not fully angelic, and thus not bound to heaven. They became restless spirits, wandering the earth, seeking embodiment.

The Book of Enoch describes them as tormenting humanity, consuming without satisfaction, and bringing violence wherever they roamed. These are the beings later called "unclean spirits" or "demons" in the New Testament... disembodied Nephilim, cursed to wander.

The Fallen Angels' Solution: Cloned Vessels

The Watchers, masters of forbidden knowledge, sought to solve this problem. They engineered bodies... cloned vessels, grown through genetic manipulation. These bodies were not born of women, but manufactured through science. They were designed to be inhabited by the wandering spirits of the Nephilim.

These vessels are what we now call the Greys:
- Uniform Appearance: Cloned bodies lack individuality, explaining the identical features of the Greys.
- Fragile Frames: Their bodies are weak, not designed for natural life but for temporary habitation.
- Large Eyes: Engineered for perception and manipulation, echoing the Watchers' obsession with forbidden sight.
- Emotionless Faces: Reflecting the absence of true soul — vessels animated only when possessed.

The Greys are not alive in the human sense. They are shells, waiting for occupation.

Demons and the Grey Connection

When most traditions speak of "demons," they are describing the disembodied spirits of the Nephilim. These spirits crave embodiment. They seek to inhabit humans, animals, or any vessel available. The Greys provide them with bodies engineered for this purpose.

Thus, the so-called "alien abduction" phenomenon is not extraterrestrial but spiritual. The Greys are vessels, and the encounters are manifestations of demonic activity. The abductions, experiments, and manipulations are continuations of the Watchers' corruption of flesh.

Ancient Parallels to the Grey Vessels

Cultures across the world preserve memory of soulless vessels:
- Golems in Jewish Lore: Bodies of clay animated by spirit, but without true soul.
- The Shedu and Lamassu: Hybrid guardians, part human, part beast, echoing engineered forms.
- The Sidhe of Celtic Tradition: Otherworldly beings who abducted humans, often described as pale, thin, and emotionless.
- The Djinn: Beings who could inhabit forms, possessing bodies not their own.

Each culture remembers the same truth: vessels created for estranged spirits, bodies without souls.

The Grey Agenda

The Greys serve the same agenda as their creators:
- Re-Embodiment of the Nephilim: Providing bodies for disembodied spirits.
- Genetic Experimentation: Continuing the corruption of flesh, blending human DNA with engineered forms.
- Surveillance of Bloodlines: Targeting families that preserve covenantal memory, seeking to infiltrate and corrupt them.
- Preparation for Deception: Presenting themselves as "aliens" to mask their true nature as vessels of estrangement.

The Grey agenda is not exploration but occupation, not curiosity but corruption.

Bloodlines Watched and Manipulated

Family bloodlines that preserve covenantal memory are prime targets for the Grey agenda. Because these families carry testimonies, genealogies, and rituals that resist estrangement, the Greys monitor them, abduct them, and attempt to experiment upon them. Their goal is not curiosity but corruption, to fracture covenantal continuity and prepare bloodlines for infiltration.

Examples of bloodlines watched and manipulated:
- Jewish rabbinic families- Preserving Torah and covenantal memory across centuries, they are targeted by deception. Reports of Grey encounters often focus on attempts to distort genealogical continuity, echoing the Watchers' ancient assault on covenantal lines.

- Christian families in persecuted regions- Preserving liturgy and testimony under suppression, they have been linked to accounts of Grey interference. The goal is to weaken covenantal endurance by sowing fear and confusion through abduction narratives.
- Messianic Jewish households- Anchoring identity in both Testaments, these families are often described as resisting manipulation. Their covenantal continuity makes them prime targets for Grey surveillance and attempted corruption.
- Monastic lineages in Eastern Christianity- Preserving prayers and archives in secrecy, they have carried testimonies of strange visitations. The Greys' agenda seeks to fracture their continuity, severing covenantal inheritance through manipulation of perception.

These families endure by:
- Anchoring themselves in GOD's Word when deception seeks to infiltrate
- Teaching children discernment against false visions and abduction narratives
- Preserving genealogies and testimonies even when targeted by manipulation

The Greys watch covenantal bloodlines because they are the living resistance. Every preserved genealogy, every remembered testimony, every prayer whispered in secrecy is a breach in estrangement's agenda.

Secret Fellowships and the Grey Question

Remnant fellowships have long discerned the truth of the Greys. They understand that the Greys are not extraterrestrials but vessels, cloned bodies engineered by fallen angel science to house disembodied Nephilim spirits. Their mission is not exploration but occupation, not discovery but deception.

Examples of fellowships confronting the Grey question:
- Early desert monastic fellowships- Recorded testimonies of demonic manifestations that echo modern Grey encounters: pale, soulless forms seeking to disrupt prayer and covenantal memory. Their chronicles warned of vessels animated by estranged spirits.
- Hidden Jewish mystical fellowships- Preserved teachings about soulless vessels, encoding warnings in symbolic language. Their discernment traditions align with the understanding that Greys are shells for wandering spirits.
- Christian pietist fellowships in Europe- Preserved testimonies of spiritual resistance, encoding warnings in hymns and prayers. Their gatherings became sanctuaries of discernment against deceptive manifestations that parallel Grey visitations.
- Underground Christian fellowships in modern authoritarian states- Report testimonies of encounters framed as "alien" but discerned as demonic. Their secrecy ensures survival, but their witness exposes the Grey agenda as spiritual warfare.

Their practices include:
- Guarding archives that encode warnings about soulless vessels
- Preserving oral traditions that teach discernment against deceptive manifestations
- Encoding truth in ritual and symbol to protect meaning from outsiders

- Bearing silent witness until deception is exposed by GOD's light

These fellowships testify that the Grey agenda can be resisted. By exposing the Greys as vessels for Nephilim spirits, they dismantle estrangement's deception. Their archives, testimonies, and rituals anchor covenantal remembrance against manipulation, ensuring that the remnant discerns and resists.

Mythic and Cultural Echoes of Vessel-Beings

- The Anakim and Rephaim: Descendants of the Nephilim, remembered as giants whose spirits lingered after death.
- The "Empty Ones" in folklore... beings without souls, animated by possession.
- Modern UFO Lore: Abductions, experiments, and hybrid programs echoing the ancient corruption of flesh.

Each culture remembers the same truth: vessels created for estranged spirits, bodies without souls.

The Remnant's Response to the Grey Interlude

The remnant resists the Grey agenda by:
- Anchoring in Scripture- discerning spirits by the Word of GOD.
- Exposing Deception- revealing the Greys as vessels, not aliens.
- Preserving Bloodlines- resisting manipulation through covenantal continuity.
- Maintaining Fellowship- resisting isolation, the weapon of abduction.

- Invoking the Name of GOD- the only authority that demons fear and obey is pronounced EHYEH, the true name of GOD given to Moshe (Moses) at the burning bush.

.

The remnant does not fear the Greys, for they are merely shells. Their power lies only in deception.

Conclusion of Chapter 18

The Grey interlude is not about extraterrestrials but about estrangement. The Greys are cloned vessels, engineered by fallen angel science, designed to house the disembodied spirits of the Nephilim. These spirits, called demons, crave embodiment, and the Greys provide it.

Yet the remnant endures. Families preserve covenant, fellowships guard memory, and the faithful anchor themselves in GOD's Word. Empires may be deceived by Greys, but the remnant discerns. Councils may conspire with them, but the remnant resists. Darkness may manifest in cloned vessels, but the remnant shines. For in the end, it is not the Greys or their parents the Watchers who prevail, but the covenant of GOD, which endures forever.

Chapter 19 -
The Great Deception

"For they are a nation void of counsel, neither is there any understanding in them. O that they were wise, that they understood this, that they would consider their latter end!"
- Deuteronomy 32:28–29

The Great Deception is not a single event. It is a convergence... of estranged technologies, spiritual manipulation, genetic corruption, and global narrative control. It is the culmination of the Watchers' rebellion, the Nephilim's re-embodiment, and the councils beneath the earth. It is the moment when deception becomes indistinguishable from truth, when the counterfeit becomes indistinguishable from the covenant with GOD. To understand the final escalation of estrangement, one must confront the Great Deception... the engineered convergence designed to enthrone the counterfeit and silence GOD's remnant.

The Anatomy of Deception

Deception is not merely a lie. It is a system that is engineered, layered, and reinforced across generations. The Great Deception is the final form of this system, a convergence of estrangement's strategies:

- Technological Illusion: Artificial intelligence, holography, and neural manipulation used to simulate divine encounters.
- Genetic Engineering: Creation of hybrid vessels (Greys and others) to house disembodied Nephilim spirits.
- Spiritual Counterfeit: False signs and wonders, designed to mimic the miraculous and deceive even the elect.
- Narrative Control: Media, education, and entertainment synchronized to reinforce the estranged worldview.
- Global Ritual: A coordinated unveiling — a "disclosure" event that presents the Greys as saviors, masking their true origin.

The deception is total. It is not just what people believe. It is what they see, feel, and experience.

The Return of the Nephilim

The Great Deception is not only technological or psychological. It is spiritual. The disembodied spirits of the Nephilim (the demons) seek embodiment. Through cloned vessels, genetic hybrids, and ritual invitation, they return.

- The Greys are their primary vessels — engineered by fallen angel science to house these spirits.

- Hybrid Programs seek to blend human DNA with Nephilim essence, creating new generations of embodied estrangement.
- Possession Rituals are disguised as "activation," "ascension," or "contact," inviting spirits into flesh.

The deception is not alien. It is ancient. It is the Watchers' rebellion reborn.

Scriptural Warnings

Scripture has always warned of this convergence:
- "There shall arise false Christs, and false prophets, and shall show great signs and wonders; insomuch that, if it were possible, they shall deceive the very elect."- Matthew 24:24
- "That day shall not come, except there come a falling away first, and that man of sin be revealed."- 2 Thessalonians 2:3
- "And no marvel; for Satan himself is transformed into an angel of light."- 2 Corinthians 11:14

The deception will be beautiful, powerful, and convincing. It will mimic light, but carry darkness.

Mythic and Cultural Echoes

Cultures across the world preserve memory of a final deception:
- The False Messiah in Jewish and Christian tradition- one who mimics the deliverer but brings destruction.
- Ragnarok's Deceiver- Loki, the trickster who engineers the final war.

- The Antichrist Archetype- a figure who unites nations, performs wonders, and demands worship.
- The "Star Visitors"- beings who promise peace, healing, and enlightenment, but conceal corruption.

Each tradition remembers the same truth: a final deception, engineered to enthrone estrangement.

Bloodlines in the Crosshairs

Family bloodlines that preserve covenantal memory are the primary targets of the Great Deception. Because they carry testimonies, genealogies, and rituals that resist estrangement, they are monitored, manipulated, and ridiculed. The Greys and their handlers seek to fracture continuity, infiltrate inheritance, and corrupt covenantal witness.

Examples of bloodlines in the crosshairs:
- Jewish families in Yemen- Preserved Torah scrolls and oral traditions under centuries of persecution. Their covenantal endurance made them prime targets for ridicule and suppression, yet their genealogical continuity resisted estrangement.
- Christian families in Cappadocia- Maintained worship in underground sanctuaries during waves of persecution. Their covenantal witness endured in secrecy, resisting manipulation and infiltration.
- Hebrew families in Alexandria- Preserved scripture and covenantal teaching in diaspora communities, resisting cultural assimilation. Their continuity became a target for distortion and ridicule by estranged powers.
- Christian families in Ireland during penal times - Preserved worship and testimony in hidden homes and

rural gatherings, resisting suppression and ridicule. Their covenantal endurance carried memory across generations despite isolation.

These families endured by:
- Anchoring memory in GOD's Word when deception sought to infiltrate
- Teaching children prayers and testimonies in secrecy
- Preserving genealogies orally when written records were destroyed
- Encoding covenantal witness in ritual and symbol when estrangement obscured history

The Great Deception seeks to isolate and fracture these families, but their endurance testifies that covenantal memory cannot be erased.

Secret Fellowships and the Warning

Remnant fellowships have long warned of the Great Deception. They preserve texts, rituals, and testimonies that expose the counterfeit. Their secrecy is not ambition but necessity, survival in the face of estrangement's convergence.

Examples of secret fellowships warning against deception:
- The Essenes at Qumran- Preserved scrolls that warned of false signs and estranged powers. Their hidden fellowship encoded discernment in scripture and ritual, preparing future generations to resist deception.
- Hidden Christian fellowships in the catacombs of Rome- Preserved testimony and worship in secrecy, resisting imperial deception that sought to enthrone counterfeit

light. Their gatherings became sanctuaries of discernment.
- Jewish mystical fellowships in medieval Europe- Encoded warnings about soulless vessels and counterfeit signs in symbolic language. Their teachings preserved discernment against deception across generations.
- Christian Brethren fellowships in Moravia- Preserved scripture and testimony in hidden communities, warning against false signs and counterfeit wonders. Their endurance testified to the seriousness of the deception.

Their practices included:
- Preserving hidden archives that describe estrangement's strategies
- Guarding oral traditions that teach discernment against counterfeit signs
- Encoding truth in ritual and symbol to protect meaning from outsiders
- Bearing silent witness until deception is exposed by GOD's light

These fellowships testify that the Great Deception can be resisted. Their archives, testimonies, and rituals anchor covenantal remembrance against manipulation, ensuring that the remnant discerns and resists.

The Role of the Greys in the Great Deception

The Greys are central to the deception:
- Presented as Saviors: Advanced beings offering healing, technology, and peace.
- Used as Signs: Their appearance and "arrival" staged to mimic divine visitation.

- Occupied by Demons: Their bodies animated by Nephilim spirits, giving them intelligence and power.
- Integrated into Religion: Reinterpreted as angels, ascended masters, or divine messengers.

Their true nature is hidden. They are not saviors. They are vessels of estrangement from GOD.

The Remnant's Weapons Against the Great Deception

The remnant resists not with force, but with faith:
- Discernment- the ability to see through signs and wonders.
- Scripture- the unchanging Word of GOD, the anchor of truth.
- Testimony- the lived witness of covenantal memory.
- Prayer and Fasting- spiritual warfare against deception.
- Fellowship- gathering in truth when isolation is enforced.

These weapons are not "flashy" to today's world, but they are eternal. They dismantle deception by remembering GOD and HIS plan for us, his children.

Conclusion of Chapter 19

The Great Deception is the final convergence of estrangement. It is the return of the Nephilim through cloned vessels. It is the enthronement of counterfeit light. It is the war not of armies, but of perception. Yet the remnant endures. Families preserve covenant, fellowships guard memory, and the faithful anchor themselves in GOD's truth.

Empires will be deceived, but the remnant will discern truth and light. Councils will conspire, but the remnant will resist them. Darkness will masquerade as light, but the remnant will shine in truth.

In the end, it is not the deception that prevails, but the truth of GOD, who does not lie, and whose covenant with his children endures forever.

Chapter 20 - Weapons of Light

"The people that walked in darkness have seen a great light: they that dwell in the land of the shadow of death, upon them hath the light shined."
- Isaiah 9:2

The deception has been exposed. The Greys revealed as vessels. The Nephilim spirits unmasked. The councils beneath the earth shaken. But exposure is not victory. The remnant must now rise... not with weapons of flesh, but with weapons of light. These are not metaphorical. They are real, spiritual technologies forged in covenant with GOD, powered by remembrance, and wielded in obedience. To confront estrangement from GOD, the remnant must be armed... not with mere swords, but with truth, testimony, and the authority of heaven.

The Nature of Light

Sometimes knowledge is referred to as light. Light in any context is not passive. It is active, invasive, and disruptive. In scripture, light is:

- Revelation: "Thy word is a lamp unto my feet" (Psalm 119:105)
- Judgment: "Men loved darkness rather than light, because their deeds were evil" (John 3:19)
- Presence: "GOD is light, and in Him is no darkness at all" (1 John 1:5)
- Weapon: "Put on the armor of light" (Romans 13:12)

Light is not merely illumination. It is confrontation. It exposes, divides, and commissions.

The Remnant's Arsenal

The remnant does not fight with earthly weapons. Their arsenal is spiritual, eternal, and precise:

- Scripture- The sword of the Spirit (Ephesians 6:17), cutting through deception and distortion.
- Testimony- The word of their witness (Revelation 12:11), lived truth that dismantles propaganda.
- Discernment- The ability to see through false signs, separating light from counterfeit.
- Prayer and Fasting- Strategic warfare that disrupts spiritual strongholds (Mark 9:29).
- Remembrance- Anchoring in covenant when deception seeks to erase history.
- Fellowship- The shield wall of the remnant, resisting isolation and fragmentation.

These weapons are not symbolic. They are tactical. They dismantle the machinery of estrangement from GOD.

Light vs. the Grey Agenda

The Greys, as cloned vessels for Nephilim spirits, operate in secrecy. Their power depends on darkness. Light disrupts them:
- Exposure- Revealing their origin dismantles their authority.
- Naming- Calling them what they are… vessels, not saviors… breaks the spell.
- Testimony- Survivors of abduction and manipulation become witnesses of truth.
- Scripture- Declaring the Word of GOD forces demonic spirits to flee.

The remnant does not fear the Greys. They confront them with light.

Bloodlines Activated

Family bloodlines that have preserved covenantal memory begin to activate in the face of deception. These lineages are not passive. They become weapons of light, carrying remembrance and testimony across generations.

Examples of bloodlines activated:
- Jewish families in Cochin, India- Preserved Torah scrolls and synagogue traditions for centuries in isolation. Their genealogical restoration in modern times became a weapon of light, reclaiming covenantal identity against estrangement.

- Christian families in Georgia (Caucasus region)-
  Maintained covenantal worship and liturgical continuity
  despite waves of invasion. Their genealogical endurance
  became a living testimony of light in a land marked by
  conflict.
- Jewish families in Morocco- Preserved covenantal rituals
  and genealogies through oral tradition, resisting
  assimilation. Their activation in remembrance became a
  shield against deception.
- Christian families in Ethiopia's highlands- Preserved
  ancient liturgical languages and genealogies, reclaiming
  continuity through ritual meals and intergenerational
  fellowship. Their activation became a weapon of
  remembrance against estrangement.
- Bloodlines are not only heritage. They are tactical. When
  genealogies are reclaimed, when names are remembered,
  when covenantal meals are enacted, families themselves
  become weapons of light.

Secret Fellowships Mobilized

Remnant fellowships move from preservation to confrontation.
Their secrecy was survival, but their activation is resistance.
These fellowships mobilize not with armies, they do it with
archives, testimonies, and coordinated prayer.

Examples of secret fellowships mobilized:
- The Karaite Jewish fellowships- Preserved scripture
  interpretation independent of rabbinic tradition, often in
  secrecy. Their mobilization became a weapon of
  discernment against deception.
- Christian desert monasteries in Nubia- Preserved scripture
  and worship in hidden sanctuaries, later mobilizing to

spread testimony across Africa. Their activation became a prophetic witness against estrangement.

- Jewish fellowships in Persia- Preserved covenantal study and ritual in clandestine gatherings, resisting suppression. Their mobilization became a shield of remembrance against deception.
- Christian Waldensian fellowships in Piedmont valleys (later mobilized openly)- Preserved scripture in secrecy, then activated networks of testimony across Europe. Their mobilization became a weapon of light against estrangement.

Their practices included:
- Releasing hidden archives of testimony and scripture
- Decoding symbols and rituals that preserved covenantal meaning
- Forming networks of families and fellowships across regions
- Coordinating prayer and fasting as strategic warfare against deception

These fellowships are not political. They are prophetic. Their weapons are light and include such things as archives, testimonies, rituals, and coordinated remembrance that dismantle estrangement's machinery.

Mythic and Cultural Echoes of Light

Cultures remember the weapons of light:
- The Sword of Nuada- A blade that only strikes truth.
- The Ark of the Covenant- A vessel of divine presence that repels darkness.
- The Lamp of Aladdin- Light that reveals hidden power.

- The Spear of Destiny- A weapon that pierces deception.

Each myth echoes the same truth: light is not passive. It is weaponized.

The Commissioning Begins

The shaking has passed. The deception is exposed. The remnant is armed. Now the commissioning begins:
- To speak when silence is enforced.
- To remember when history is erased.
- To gather when isolation is mandated.
- To shine when darkness masquerades as light.

The remnant is not waiting. They are rising.

Conclusion of Chapter 20

Weapons of light are not poetic. They are tactical. They are the arsenal of the remnant, forged in covenant, powered by remembrance, and wielded in obedience. The deception has been exposed. The shaking has begun. The remnant is armed.

Empires will tremble, but the remnant will stand. Councils will fracture, but the remnant will remember. Darkness will rage, but the remnant will shine. For in the end, it is not deception that prevails, but the light of GOD... eternal, unbreakable, and victorious.

Chapter 21 -
The Collapse of Their Net

"He disappointeth the devices of the crafty, so that their hands cannot perform their enterprise."
- Job 5:12

The net was vast. Woven from deception, ritual, technology, and control. It spanned nations, institutions, and generations. But it is collapsing. Not all at once, but in fractures... cracks in the machinery, ruptures in the narrative, awakenings in the bloodlines. The remnant has risen, and the weapons of light have begun to tear through the veil. The councils beneath the earth tremble. The Greys are exposed. The deception falters. And around the world, signs emerge that the war is being won.

The Net Defined

The "net" is not metaphor. It is the engineered system of estrangement from GOD:
- Technological Surveillance: Algorithms designed to monitor, manipulate, and isolate.
- Narrative Control: Media and academia synchronized to enforce the estranged worldview.
- Genetic Manipulation: Hybrid programs designed to corrupt flesh and sever covenant.
- Spiritual Counterfeit: False signs and wonders engineered to mimic divine truth.
- Global Ritual: Coordinated deception masquerading as progress, unity, or enlightenment.

This net was designed to entrap the remnant, suppress memory, and enthrone estrangement.

Modern Fractures in the Net

Around the world, the net is collapsing. Not in silence, but in spectacle.

1. Exposure of AI-Driven Disinformation
- Investigations have revealed how artificial intelligence is used to generate false narratives, manipulate elections, and distort truth.
- Yet whistleblowers, journalists, and technologists are fighting back... exposing the algorithms, demanding transparency, and building counter-networks.
2. Collapse of Centralized Fact-Control
- Meta's decision to end its third-party fact-checking program has backfired.

- Instead of silencing dissent, it has triggered mass awakening . Users now question everything, seek original sources, and rediscover forgotten truths.

3. Global Resistance to Authoritarian Narratives
- In multiple nations, citizens are rejecting centralized control, demanding sovereignty, and reviving ancestral traditions.
- Indigenous movements, family archives, and spiritual fellowships are resurfacing... not as nostalgia, but as resistance.

4. Military Countermeasures Against Digital Deception
- NATO exercises now include disinformation warfare training.
- The battlefield has shifted, and truth is now a strategic weapon.

These fractures are not isolated. They are coordinated, and the remnant is rising.

Bloodlines Breaking the Net

Family bloodlines that preserve covenantal memory are now active. These lineages, once hidden, are rising to confront estrangement. Their genealogies, testimonies, and rituals are becoming weapons of light, breaking the net of deception.

Examples of bloodlines breaking the net:
- Jewish families in Aleppo (Syria)- Preserved fragments of the Aleppo Codex and oral traditions through centuries of upheaval. Their restoration of scripture and memory became a weapon of light against suppression.

- Christian families in the Chaldean tradition (Iraq)- Maintained liturgical continuity and genealogical remembrance despite waves of war and displacement. Their endurance now emerges as testimony against estrangement.
- Jewish families in Thessaloniki (Greece)- Preserved covenantal rituals and genealogies even after devastation in the Holocaust. Their reclamation of memory and restoration of lineage breaks the net of erasure.
- Christian recusant families in Scotland- Preserved worship and testimony in secrecy during centuries of suppression. Their genealogical restoration now becomes a living archive of resistance.

These families break the net by:
- Sharing testimonies once hidden in secrecy
- Restoring genealogies erased by empire and war
- Reinterpreting symbols and heirlooms as covenantal weapons
- Activating children through dreams, visions, and spiritual gifts

The councils beneath the earth cannot silence them. The bloodlines are speaking, and their voices fracture the net.

Secret Fellowships Disrupting the Net

Many remnant fellowships are no longer hidden. They are strategic, prophetic, and mobilized. Their archives, rituals, and networks are dismantling estrangement's machinery, breaking the net from within.

Examples of fellowships disrupting the net:

- The Karaite Jewish fellowships in Crimea- Preserved scripture and covenantal study outside rabbinic authority, resisting suppression. Their release of archives now disrupts deception by reclaiming truth.
- Christian Hussite fellowships in Bohemia- Preserved scripture and worship in clandestine circles, resisting both empire and ecclesiastical suppression. Their mobilization became a prophetic disruption of estrangement.
- Jewish fellowships in Amsterdam during the diaspora- Preserved hidden archives and testimonies of exile, later publishing them to expose deception. Their mobilization became a weapon of remembrance.
- Christian Pietist fellowships in Scandinavia- Preserved worship and testimony in small circles, resisting state suppression. Their mobilization now disrupts estrangement by restoring covenantal fellowship.

Their practices include:
- Releasing archives once sealed in secrecy
- Forming networks across continents to resist isolation
- Restoring rituals of covenantal meals, songs, and symbols
- Mobilizing prayer as coordinated spiritual warfare

These fellowships are not reactive. They are prophetic. Their light is strategic, and their disruption ensures that the net collapses under the weight of truth.

Mythic Echoes of Net Collapse

Cultures remember the collapse of false systems:
- The Fall of Babel- language fractured, unity dismantled.

- The Breaking of the Matrix- illusion shattered, reality restored.
- The Unmasking of Loki- the deceiver exposed before Ragnarok.
- The Veil Torn in the Temple- separation ended, truth revealed.

Each myth echoes the same truth: the net cannot hold when light breaks through.

The Remnant's Role in the Collapse

The remnant is not passive. They are the catalysts of collapse.
- By speaking truth when silence is enforced.
- By remembering when history is erased.
- By gathering when isolation is mandated.
- By shining when darkness masquerades as light.

Many of their weapons are not of this world. They are eternal. And they are working.

Conclusion of Chapter 21

The net of estrangement is collapsing. Around the world, deception is exposed, bloodlines are awakened, fellowships are mobilized, and truth is rising. The remnant is not waiting. They are acting. And the councils beneath the earth tremble.

Empires will fall, but the remnant will stand. Algorithms will fail, but the remnant will remember. Darkness will rage, but the remnant will shine. For in the end, it is not the net that prevails, but the light of GOD ... eternal, unbreakable, and victorious.

Chapter 22 -
Fire From Heaven and Victory

"Then the fire of the LORD fell, and consumed the burnt sacrifice, and the wood, and the stones, and the dust, and licked up the water that was in the trench."

- 1 Kings 18:38

There comes a moment when remembrance is no longer resistance, but vindication. When the remnant, having stood in truth, is answered not by signs of deception, but by fire from heaven. This is not metaphor. It is judgment. It is the collapse of estrangement's altars, the silencing of counterfeit prophets, and the restoration of covenant.

The fire does not yet fall on the deceivers... it falls on the altar of the remnant, consuming their offering, confirming the truth, and declaring victory.

The Pattern of Fire

Scripture reveals a consistent pattern: when deception reaches its peak, fire falls:
- Elijah on Mount Carmel: The prophets of Baal cried all day. Elijah rebuilt the altar, poured water on the sacrifice, and prayed. Fire fell. Truth was vindicated (1 Kings 18).
- Sodom and Gomorrah: When corruption reached its fullness, fire fell from heaven (Genesis 19).
- Pentecost: Tongues of fire fell on the faithful, not in judgment, but in commissioning (Acts 2).
- Revelation: Fire proceeds from the mouth of the witnesses, consuming their enemies (Revelation 11:5).

Fire is not destruction. It is decision. It separates truth from deception. The river that flows beneath GOD's throne is not water, but a river of fire.

The Remnant's Altar

The remnant does not build altars of stone. They build altars of memory, testimony, and obedience:
- Memory- preserving what was forgotten.
- Testimony- speaking what was silenced.
- Obedience- standing when others kneel.

This altar is not visible to the world. But heaven sees it. And when the time is right, fire will fall.

Modern Echoes of Fire

Around the world, signs of divine disruption are emerging. They are emerging not as chaos, but as confrontation.

1. Exposure of Ritual Abuse Networks
   - Hidden systems of exploitation, long protected by media and institutions, are being exposed.
   - Survivors are speaking. Documents are surfacing. The altars of estrangement are burning.

2. Collapse of False Prophets
   - Influencers and spiritual leaders who once claimed divine authority are being unmasked.
   - Their teachings are revealed as plagiarized, manipulated, or engineered for control.

3. Unexplainable Signs
   - Fireballs, sky anomalies, and atmospheric disruptions are increasing.
   - Scientists offer explanations. But the remnant discerns patterns and signs of confrontation.

4. Revival in Unexpected Places
   - In prisons, refugee camps, and underground fellowships, the Spirit is moving.
   - Not through spectacle, but through remembrance, repentance, and restoration.

These are not random. They are fire from heaven and are answering the remnant's altar.

Bloodlines Vindicated

Families that preserved covenantal memory are now being vindicated. Their traditions, once mocked, are honored. Their genealogies, once erased, are restored. Their testimonies, once silenced, are published. The fire from heaven confirms their endurance.

Examples of bloodlines vindicated:
- Jewish families in Djerba (Tunisia)- Preserved Torah scrolls and covenantal rituals for centuries in isolation. Their traditions, once dismissed as relics, are now recognized as living testimony of GOD's covenant.
- Christian families in the Mar Thoma tradition (Kerala, India)- Maintained apostolic continuity through liturgy and genealogy despite colonial disruption. Their witness, once marginalized, is now honored as a sign of endurance.
- Jewish families in the Caucasus (Mountain Jews)- Preserved covenantal identity through oral tradition and hidden archives. Their genealogies, once ignored, are now restored as testimony of GOD's faithfulness.
- Christian families in the Assyrian diaspora- Preserved liturgical memory and genealogical continuity across displacement. Their testimonies, once silenced, are now published as witness against estrangement.

These families show that fire from heaven is vindication. Their endurance is confirmation that covenantal memory cannot be erased.

Secret Fellowships Commissioned

Remnant fellowships are no longer remaining hidden. They are being commissioned to speak, preserve, gather, and confront. Their secrecy was survival, but their commissioning is victory. Examples of secret fellowships commissioned:

- Jewish study fellowships in Vilna (Lithuania)- Preserved Torah learning in secrecy during persecution. Now their archives are released, their memory restored, and their fellowship commissioned to speak openly.
- Christian Moravian fellowships in Herrnhut (Germany)- Preserved worship and testimony in hidden circles. Now their networks are mobilized, their archives published, and their fellowship commissioned to confront estrangement boldly.
- Jewish fellowships in Baghdad (Iraq)- Preserved covenantal rituals in secrecy during centuries of suppression. Now their testimonies are honored, their genealogies restored, and their fellowship commissioned to preserve memory openly.
- Christian underground fellowships in China- Preserved worship in secrecy under authoritarian suppression. Now their gatherings are rising, their testimonies shared, and their fellowship commissioned to confront estrangement with boldness.

These fellowships testify that fire from heaven is commissioning.

Their endurance is transformed into boldness, their secrecy into proclamation, their preservation into confrontation.

Mythic and Cultural Echoes of Victory

Cultures remember the moment of divine fire:
- Prometheus- fire stolen from the gods, but later reclaimed by truth.
- The Phoenix- consumed in flame, but reborn in light.
- The Burning Bush- fire that does not consume, but commissions.

- The Spear of Destiny- a weapon that pierces deception and confirms truth.

Each myth echoes the same truth: fire is not the end. It is the beginning of victory.

The Remnant's Victory

Victory is not conquest. It is confirmation:
- The deception is exposed.
- The bloodlines endure.
- The fellowships rise.
- The altar is answered.

The remnant does not gloat. They remember. They do not dominate. They preserve. They do not retaliate. They restore.

Conclusion of Chapter 22

Fire from heaven is not destruction. It is decision. It is the moment when the remnant's altar is answered, when deception is consumed, and when truth is vindicated. Around the world, signs are emerging. The net is collapsing. The councils are trembling. The remnant is rising.

Empires will fall, but the remnant will stand. Thrones will burn, but the altar will endure. Darkness will rage, but the fire will fall.

For in the end, it is not estrangement that prevails, but the covenant with GOD... eternal, unbreakable, and victorious.

Conclusion -
Call to Arms

"Blow ye the trumpet in Zion, and sound an alarm in My holy mountain: let all the inhabitants of the land tremble: for the day of the LORD cometh, for it is nigh at hand."
- Joel 2:1

The War Was Never Fiction

You have read of the descent. You have seen the machinery. You have traced the bloodlines, decoded the symbols, and watched the deception fracture. This was never mythology. It was memory. It was never fiction. It was testimony. The war was never distant. It was here in front of every person... in your calendar, your language, your body, your family.

The Watchers fell. The Nephilim corrupted. The Greys were engineered. The councils beneath the earth conspired. But the remnant endured. And now, the altar has been answered. The fire has started falling. The deception is exposed.

You Are the Remnant

If you remember, you are the remnant.
If you resist, you are the remnant.
If you preserve truth when others erase it, you are the remnant.
If you speak when silence is enforced, you are the remnant.

If you gather when isolation is mandated, you are the remnant. If you shine when darkness masquerades as light, you are the remnant.

You are not alone. You are not powerless. You are not forgotten. You are commissioned.

The Commissioning

This is your call to arms. Not to violence… but to remembrance. Not to conquest… but to covenant:
- Speak truth in your home, your fellowship, your archive.
- Preserve memory in your bloodline, your rituals, your testimony.
- Break deception with scripture, discernment, and light.
- Guard the altar with obedience, not spectacle.
- Prepare the way for the return of the Kingdom of GOD.

You are not waiting for rescue. You are preparing for restoration.

The Time Is Now

The shaking has begun. The deception is collapsing. The fire has started to fall. The remnant is rising.

Empires will fall. Thrones will burn. Councils will fracture. But the covenant will endure. The memory will survive. The remnant will shine.

You are not reading a book. You are holding a commission.
You are not finishing a story. You are stepping into one.
Blow the trumpet. Sound the alarm, because the day is near.
The war is being won, and you are to be witness to it.

Appendix -
Master Bibliography of Sources

This consolidated bibliography gathers all verifiable references cited across Chapters 1–22. It is organized by Chapter for clarity.

Chapter 1 Sources

Scriptural Sources
• Genesis 6:1-4 - "sons of GOD" and the Nephilim
• Deuteronomy 32:8-9 - division of nations under divine beings
• Psalm 82 - GOD judging the divine council
• Jude 1:6 - angels who left their first estate
• 2 Peter 2:4 - angels bound in chains of darkness
Ancient / Apocryphal Sources
• 1 Enoch 6-8 - descent of the Watchers, oath on Hermon, forbidden teachings
• Jubilees 5 - corruption of flesh and judgment
• Dead Sea Scrolls (Book of Giants) - fragments on Nephilim offspring

Comparative Mythology
• Mesopotamian Apkallu - semi-divine sages teaching forbidden arts
• Greek Titanomachy - divine rebellion and binding in Tartarus
• Norse Jotnar - giants opposing the gods
Modern Scholarship
• Michael Heiser, Reversing Hermon
• Annette Yoshiko Reed, Fallen Angels and the History of Judaism and Christianity
• Loren Stuckenbruck, The Book of Giants from Qumran

Chapter 2 Sources

Scriptural Sources
• Jeremiah 6:14 - "they cry peace when there is no peace"
• Daniel 7 - beasts as empires
• Revelation 13 - the Beast system of control

Ancient / Historical Sources
- Egyptian monuments and priestly control systems
- Babylonian ziggurats and priestly calendars
- Roman imperial cult and propaganda

Comparative Mythology
- Enuma Elish - divine kingship and order through violence
- Zoroastrian daevas - false rulers of nations

Modern Scholarship
- Aldous Huxley, Brave New World
- Shoshana Zuboff, The Age of Surveillance Capitalism
- Jacques Ellul, The Technological Society

Chapter 3 Sources

Scriptural Sources
- Genesis 6:12 - "all flesh corrupted"
- Deuteronomy 2-3 - Anakim, Rephaim, Zamzummim
- 1 Samuel 17 - Goliath of Gath
- Genesis 4:22 - Tubal-Cain, metallurgy

Ancient / Apocryphal Sources
- 1 Enoch 7-8 - Watchers teaching metallurgy, enchantments
- Jubilees 4 - Cain's descendants and crafts
- Dead Sea Scrolls (Book of Giants)

Comparative Mythology
- Greek demigods (Heracles, Perseus)
- Mesopotamian Apkallu
- Hindu Nagas and Asuras
- Mesoamerican feathered serpent rulers

Modern Scholarship
- Mircea Eliade, The Forge and the Crucible
- Michael Heiser, The Unseen Realm
- David Jacobs, The Threat (abduction/hybridization research)

Chapter 4 Sources

Scriptural Sources
- Psalm 2:2 - "the kings of the earth take counsel together"
- Deuteronomy 32:8-9 - divine allotment of nations
- Job 1–2 - heavenly council scenes

Ancient / Apocryphal Sources
- 1 Enoch 6-16 - Watchers' oath and councils
- Jubilees 5 - corruption and judgment
- Dead Sea Scrolls (Book of Giants)

Comparative Mythology
- Ugaritic Baal Cycle - divine council of El
- Greek Boule and Roman Senate - councils of rulers with divine claims
- Mesoamerican priest-kings and blood councils

Modern Scholarship
- Mark S. Smith, The Origins of Biblical Monotheism
- Michael Heiser, The Divine Council in Second Temple Literature

Chapter 5 Sources

Scriptural Sources
- James 4:2 - "ye lust and have not, ye fight and war"
- 1 Enoch 8:1 - Azazel teaching weaponry

- Isaiah 2:4 - swords into plowshares

Ancient / Historical Sources
- Assyrian war inscriptions (ritualized conquest)
- Roman triumphs as sacrificial ritual
- Aztec "flower wars" for sacrificial victims

Comparative Mythology
- Homer's Iliad - war as divine ritual
- Norse Ragnarok - final war as cosmic liturgy

Modern Scholarship
- Mircea Eliade, The Sacred and the Profane
- Jonathan Z. Smith, To Take Place
- Studies on the "military-industrial complex"

Chapter 6 Sources

Scriptural Sources
- Revelation 18:23 - "by thy sorceries were all nations deceived"
- Galatians 5:20 - pharmakeia as work of the flesh
- Revelation 9:21 - refusal to repent of sorceries

Ancient / Apocryphal Sources
- 1 Enoch 7–8 — Watchers teaching root-cutting and enchantments
- Greek Magical Papyri — spells and potions
- Babylonian incantation bowls

Comparative Mythology
- Egyptian temple potions and rituals
- Greek mystery cults (Eleusis)
- Medieval alchemy

Modern Scholarship
- John Allegro, Sacred Mushroom and the Cross
- Carl Ruck, The Road to Eleusis
- Richard Dolan, The Secret Space Program and Breakaway Civilization

Chapter 7 Sources

Scriptural Sources
- Isaiah 10:20-22 - "a remnant shall return"
- Romans 11:5 - "a remnant according to the election of grace"
- Revelation 12:17 - the dragon makes war with the remnant

Ancient / Apocryphal Sources
- Qumran Community Rule (1QS) - sectarian remnant identity
- 2 Baruch 78-87 - remnant preserved through judgment

Comparative Mythology
- Norse "hidden folk" surviving Ragnarök
- Hopi prophecies of the faithful who endure the purification

Modern Scholarship
- Dietrich Bonhoeffer, Life Together
- Francis Schaeffer, How Should We Then Live?
- N.T. Wright, Paul and the Faithfulness of GOD

Chapter 8 Sources

Scriptural Sources
- Deuteronomy 6:4-9, The Holy Bible.
- Revelation 12:11, The Holy Bible.
- Psalm 119:11, The Holy Bible.

- Exodus 12:14, The Holy Bible.
- Luke 22:19, The Holy Bible.

Ancient / Apocryphal Sources
- Passover Haggadah. Traditional Jewish liturgy.
- Homeric Hymns. Translated by Hugh G. Evelyn-White.
- Dead Sea Scrolls. Qumran community texts, c. 2nd century BCE - 1st century CE.
- Early Christian house church practices, documented in Didache and patristic writings.

Comparative Mythology
- Celtic bardic traditions, preserved in oral verse.
- Native American oral traditions, e.g., Lakota storytelling cycles.
- African Griot genealogical traditions, West Africa.
- Druidic oral traditions resisting Roman assimilation.

Modern Scholarship
- Jan Assmann, Cultural Memory and Early Civilization: Writing, Remembrance, and Political Imagination. Cambridge University Press, 2011.
- Yosef Hayim Yerushalmi, Zakhor: Jewish History and Jewish Memory. University of Washington Press, 1982.
- Walter J. Ong, Orality and Literacy: The Technologizing of the Word. Routledge, 1982.
- John S. Mbiti, African Religions and Philosophy. Heinemann, 1969.

Chapter 9 Sources

Scriptural Sources
- Daniel 7:25, The Holy Bible.

- Ecclesiastes 3, The Holy Bible.
- Genesis 2:3, The Holy Bible.
- Leviticus 23, The Holy Bible.

Ancient / Apocryphal Sources
- Mayan Long Count calendar, Popol Vuh traditions.
- Roman Julian calendar reforms, Julius Caesar, 46 BCE.
- Gregorian calendar reform, Pope Gregory XIII, 1582.
- Book of Jubilees. Translated by R.H. Charles.
- Babylonian captivity and calendrical disruption, documented in 2 Kings and Ezra.

Comparative Mythology
- Hindu Yugas, cyclical ages of decline and renewal.
- Norse Ragnarök, mythic reset of time.
- Indigenous traditions of "time before time," e.g., Hopi cosmology.
- Chinese dynastic cycles and the Mandate of Heaven.

Modern Scholarship
- David F. Noble, The Religion of Technology: The Divinity of Man and the Spirit of Invention. Knopf, 1997.
- Eviatar Zerubavel, Hidden Rhythms: Schedules and Calendars in Social Life. University of California Press, 1981.
- Fiona Broome, Mandela Effect Archives. Online testimonies, 2009-present.
- Anthony Aveni, Empires of Time: Calendars, Clocks, and Cultures. University Press of Colorado, 2002.
- Sacha Stern, Calendars in Antiquity: Empires, States, and Societies. Oxford University Press, 2012.

Chapter 10 Sources

Scriptural Sources
• Genesis 11:7 - "Come, let Us go down, and there confound their language…"
• Genesis 11:1-9 - Tower of Babel narrative
• Isaiah 40:8 - "The word of our God shall stand forever"
• John 1:1 - "In the beginning was the Word…"
• James 3:5-6 - The tongue as a fire

Ancient / Apocryphal Sources
• Egyptian hieroglyphic priestly traditions - literacy controlled by elites
• Babylonian incantation texts - language as binding spells
• Greek Sophists - rhetorical manipulation of truth
• Roman imperial edicts - laws written to obscure clarity
• Medieval Catholic prohibitions on vernacular scripture (Council of Toulouse, 1229)

Comparative Mythology
• Vedic oral tradition in India - preservation of sacred language across millennia
• Qur'an recitation in Arabic - cadence preserved against translation
• Torah reading in Hebrew - covenant anchored in sacred tongue
• Indigenous chants and songs - oral preservation of covenantal memory
• Sumerian incantations and Akkadian texts - early examples of language as power

Modern Scholarship

- Jacques Derrida, Of Grammatology - deconstruction and instability of meaning
- George Orwell, Politics and the English Language - critique of linguistic corruption
- Walter J. Ong, Orality and Literacy: The Technologizing of the Word- transition from oral to written culture
- Noam Chomsky, Manufacturing Consent: The Political Economy of the Mass Media- propaganda and control of language
- Jan Assmann, Cultural Memory and Early Civilization - language as vessel of remembrance

Chapter 11 Sources

Scriptural Sources
- Isaiah 59:14 - "Truth is fallen in the street, and equity cannot enter."
- 2 Timothy 2:9 - "The word of God is not bound."
- Amos 8:11–12 - prophecy of famine for hearing the words of the LORD
- Matthew 10:27 - "What I tell you in darkness, speak ye in light."
- Acts 4:20 - "For we cannot but speak the things which we have seen and heard."

Ancient / Apocryphal Sources
- Egyptian priestly restrictions on sacred texts - literacy confined to elites
- Babylonian scribal chronicles - rewriting history to glorify kings
- Roman censorship edicts - silencing dissent and outlawing testimony
- Medieval Inquisitions - burning manuscripts and enforcing silence through terror

- Crypto-Jewish (Converso) practices - hidden rituals under the Spanish Inquisition

Comparative Mythology
- Greek "Damnatio Memoriae" - erasing names from monuments to obliterate memory
- Qin dynasty "Burning of Books" - suppression of dissenting philosophies in China
- Soviet erasures - altered photographs, deleted names, rewritten histories
- Armenian oral testimonies of genocide - preserved despite systematic silencing
- Romani oral traditions - genealogies and songs carried despite marginalization

Modern Scholarship
- Aleksandr Solzhenitsyn, The Gulag Archipelago - testimony against enforced silence
- Michel Foucault, Discipline and Punish - mechanisms of suppression and control
- Václav Havel, The Power of the Powerless - resistance to censorship in totalitarian regimes
- Anne Applebaum, Gulag: A History - documenting silenced testimonies
- Eric Metaxas, Bonhoeffer: Pastor, Martyr, Prophet, Spy - witness against Nazi silence

Chapter 12 Sources

Scriptural Sources
- Proverbs 25:2 - "It is the glory of GOD to conceal a thing..."
- Genesis 41 - Joseph preserving grain in Egypt during famine
- Ezra 7 - Ezra and the scribes preserving the Law after exile

- Jeremiah 36 - Baruch preserving prophetic testimony despite royal attempts to destroy it
- Acts 2 - Apostles preserving and proclaiming the words of Yeshuah

Ancient / Apocryphal Sources
- Syriac Christian manuscripts - preserved in Mesopotamia under imperial pressure
- Coptic liturgical fragments - preserved in Egypt against assimilation
- Yemenite Jewish Torah scrolls - preserved in secrecy across centuries
- Hawaiian oral genealogies - preserved through chants despite colonial suppression
- Nestorian archives - preserved in Persia and carried eastward into Asia

Comparative Mythology
- Essenes at Qumran - scrolls hidden in caves, later discovered as the Dead Sea Scrolls
- Irish monks - preserving scripture during the Dark Ages
- African Griots - genealogies preserved through song and oral tradition
- Indigenous elders in the Arctic - preserving sacred stories in hidden gatherings
- Bogomil fellowships in the Balkans - safeguarding scripture against suppression

Modern Scholarship
- Geza Vermes, The Complete Dead Sea Scrolls in English - study of hidden preservation at Qumran
- Thomas Cahill, How the Irish Saved Civilization - preservation of scripture by Irish monks

- Jan Vansina, Oral Tradition as History - study of oral preservation in African societies
- John Boswell, The Bogomil Heresy - fellowship preservation in the Balkans
- David Crystal, Language Death - modern preservation against linguistic and cultural erasure

Chapter 13 Sources

Scriptural Sources
- Deuteronomy 8:2 - remembrance through wilderness testing
- Genesis 18 - Abraham's covenantal feast with the three visitors
- Exodus 12 - institution of the Passover meal
- Exodus 24:9–11 - Moses and the elders eating before GOD on Sinai
- Luke 22:19–20 - institution of the Lord's Supper

Ancient / Apocryphal Sources
- Rabbinic Passover traditions - ritualized remembrance at the table
- Early Christian Eucharistic liturgies - covenantal meals in house churches
- Ethiopian Orthodox fasting and feasting cycles - covenantal rhythm preserved in meals
- Maroon feasts in the Caribbean - remembrance of deliverance from slavery
- Pacific Islander harvest feasts - covenantal meals tied to ocean and land cycle

Comparative Mythology
- Greek Symposia - feasts blending philosophy and ritual
- Norse Blots - sacrificial feasts binding clans in covenant

- Indigenous feasts in the Andes - meals shared in remembrance of ancestors
- Waldensian hidden feasts - covenantal meals preserved in secrecy
- Quaker communal meals - simplicity and testimony preserved at the table

Modern Scholarship
- Andrew McGowan, Ancient Christian Worship: Early Church Practices in Social Context - study of covenantal meals
- Gordon J. Wenham, The Book of Leviticus - commentary on feasts and covenantal meals
- Walter Brueggemann, Theology of the Old Testament - covenantal remembrance in ritual practice
- Caroline Walker Bynum, Holy Feast and Holy Fast - medieval covenantal meals and fasting traditions
- John Koenig, The Feast of the World's Redemption - Eucharistic theology and covenantal remembrance

Chapter 14 Sources

Scriptural Sources
- Isaiah 5:20 - "Woe unto them that call evil good, and good evil..."
- Jeremiah 23:16 - warning against false prophets who speak deception
- Matthew 24:24 - prophecy of false Christs and false prophets deceiving many
- 2 Thessalonians 2:9–10 - deception through signs and lying wonders
- Revelation 12:9 - the deceiver of the whole world

Ancient / Apocryphal Sources

- Egyptian priesthood rituals - cloaking idolatry in divine order
- Babylonian astrology texts - binding nations to stars rather than covenantal time
- Greek sophistry - elevating rhetoric above truth
- Roman imperial propaganda - emperors declared divine to sanctify tyranny
- Platonic allegory of the cave - shadows mistaken for reality

Comparative Mythology
- Hindu concept of Maya - the world as illusion, truth hidden beneath deception
- Trickster figures in folklore - deceivers manipulating perception (e.g., Coyote in Native American traditions)
- Norse Loki - god of mischief and deception, fracturing fellowship through lies
- Prophetic denunciations - Isaiah, Jeremiah, and others warning against lying priests
- Indigenous South American myths - deceivers who distort ancestral memory

Modern Scholarship
- Edward Bernays, Propaganda - foundational text on engineered deception in modern society
- Neil Postman, Amusing Ourselves to Death - media as an engine of distortion
- Aldous Huxley, Brave New World - dystopian vision of systemic deception
- Jacques Ellul, Propaganda: The Formation of Men's Attitudes - analysis of deception as system
- Shoshana Zuboff, The Age of Surveillance Capitalism - digital platforms as engines of manipulation

Chapter 15 Sources

Scriptural Sources
- Daniel 7:25 - prophecy of changing times and laws
- Exodus 20:8 - "Remember the Sabbath day, to keep it holy"
- Deuteronomy 8:2 - remembrance of GOD's leading in the wilderness
- Luke 22:19 - "This do in remembrance of Me"
- Malachi 3:6 - "I am the LORD, I change not"

Ancient / Apocryphal Sources
- Samaritan Torah traditions - genealogical continuity preserved in secrecy
- Assyrian Christian prayers - oral testimonies preserved in Aramaic
- Māori whakapapa - genealogical chants preserved against colonial suppression
- Greek Lethe - river of forgetfulness in Hades
- Norse Yggdrasil - tree of memory threatened by chaos

Comparative Mythology
- Hindu Maya - illusion veiling true reality
- Indigenous Pacific Northwest oral histories - stories of "time before time"
- Holocaust-era Jewish fellowships - testimonies preserved in secrecy against erasure
- Cathar fellowships in medieval France - archives preserved against ecclesiastical suppression
- Polish Catholic oral traditions - testimonies preserved under communist propaganda

Modern Scholarship
- Fiona Broome, Mandela Effect Archives - collection of testimonies on fractured memory
- Elizabeth Loftus, The Myth of Repressed Memory - psychological study of false memory
- Frederic Bartlett, Remembering: A Study in Experimental and Social Psychology - foundational work on collective memory
- Shoshana Zuboff, The Age of Surveillance Capitalism - manipulation of perception through digital systems
- Jan Assmann, Cultural Memory and Early Civilization - covenantal memory as cultural anchor

Chapter 16 Sources

Scriptural Sources
- Isaiah 14:9-11 - council of the dead
- Ezekiel 32 - kings of the nations in Sheol
- Revelation 9 - abyss and locust-like beings
- Psalm 64:6 - hidden plotting in the depths

Ancient / Apocryphal Sources
- Mesopotamian underworld councils
- Greek Hades assemblies
- 1 Enoch 10-18 - Watchers bound beneath the earth
- Jubilees - traditions of angelic rebellion and judgment

Comparative Mythology
- Mayan Xibalba lords
- Norse Hel's council
- Celtic Sidhe courts beneath hollow hills
- Mesoamerican Popol Vuh - trials in the underworld

Modern Scholarship
- Peter Levenda, Sinister Forces
- Richard Dolan, UFOs and the National Security State
- Mircea Eliade, Myth and Reality
- Jeffrey Burton Russell, The Devil: Perceptions of Evil from Antiquity to Primitive Christianity

Chapter 17 Sources

Scriptural Sources
- Revelation 12:7-9 - war in heaven
- Daniel 10 — angelic conflict

Ancient / Apocryphal Sources
- Mahabharata - celestial weapons
- Norse Ragnarok battles

Comparative Mythology
- Zoroastrian dualism - cosmic war
- Hopi prophecies of purification war

Modern Scholarship
- Nick Cook, The Hunt for Zero Point
- Joseph Farrell, The Cosmic War

Chapter 18 Sources

Scriptural Sources
- Genesis 6:4 - Nephilim
- Jude 1:6 - angels bound in chains

Ancient / Apocryphal Sources
• Djinn traditions in Islamic lore
• Celtic Sidhe abductions

Comparative Mythology
• Jewish golem - soulless vessel
• Shinto yokai abductions

Modern Scholarship
• John Keel, The Mothman Prophecies
• David Jacobs, Walking Among Us

Chapter 19 Sources

Scriptural Sources
• 2 Thessalonians 2 - man of lawlessness
• Matthew 24:24 - false signs and wonders

Ancient / Apocryphal Sources
• False messiah traditions in Judaism
• Loki's deception before Ragnarok

Comparative Mythology
• Hindu Kalki counterfeit prophecies
• Mesoamerican Quetzalcoatl return myths

Modern Scholarship
• Hal Lindsey, The Late Great Planet Earth
• Gary Bates, Alien Intrusion

Chapter 20 Sources

Scriptural Sources
- Isaiah 9:2 - "The people that walked in darkness have seen a great light."
- Romans 13:12 - "Let us put on the armor of light."
- Ephesians 6:10-18 - the full armor of GOD.
- John 1:5 - "The light shineth in darkness; and the darkness comprehended it not."
- Revelation 12:11 - "They overcame him by the blood of the Lamb, and by the word of their testimony."

Ancient / Apocryphal Sources
- 1 Enoch 108 - the righteous clothed in light.
- Dead Sea Scrolls (War Scroll, 1QM) - "Sons of Light" vs. "Sons of Darkness."
- Jubilees 23 - light as covenantal inheritance.

Comparative Mythology
- Celtic Tuatha Dé Danann - wielders of shining weapons (Sword of Nuada).
- Norse myth - Baldr, the shining god, as symbol of purity and light.
- Zoroastrian dualism - Ahura Mazda's light vs. Angra Mainyu's darkness.

Modern / Scholarly Sources
- C.S. Lewis, The Screwtape Letters (light as resistance to deception).
- Derek Prince, They Shall Expel Demons (practical spiritual warfare).

- N.T. Wright, Paul and the Faithfulness of GOD (armor of GOD in context).
- Studies on nonviolent resistance (e.g., Gene Sharp, From Dictatorship to Democracy) - remembrance and truth as weapons.

Chapter 21 Sources

<u>Scriptural Sources</u>
- Job 5:12-13 - "He disappointeth the devices of the crafty."
- Psalm 141:10 - "Let the wicked fall into their own nets."
- Isaiah 25:7 - "He will destroy...the covering cast over all people."
- Habakkuk 1:15-17 - nations caught in the net of empire.

<u>Ancient / Apocryphal Sources</u>
- 1 Enoch 56 - binding of the fallen ones in nets of judgment.
- Dead Sea Scrolls (Pesher Habakkuk) - condemnation of the "Wicked Priest" and his net of lies.
- Greek myth of Hephaestus' net - ensnaring adulterous gods.

<u>Comparative Mythology</u>
- Norse Loki caught in a net before Ragnarok.
- Hindu Indra's Net - cosmic web of illusion and entrapment.
- Hopi prophecies - "the web of lies will break."

<u>Modern / Scholarly Sources</u>
- Shoshana Zuboff, The Age of Surveillance Capitalism (digital nets of control).
- Edward Snowden, Permanent Record (exposure of surveillance systems).
- Jacques Vallée, Messengers of Deception (control systems disguised as contact).

- Contemporary examples:
- Collapse of centralized censorship regimes (e.g., social media fact-checking failures).
- Whistleblower revelations exposing hidden networks.
- Global resistance movements reclaiming sovereignty and memory.

Chapter 22 Sources

Scriptural Sources
- 1 Kings 18:38 - Elijah on Mount Carmel, fire consuming the sacrifice.
- Genesis 19:24 - fire and brimstone on Sodom and Gomorrah.
- Acts 2:3 - tongues of fire at Pentecost.
- Revelation 11:5 - fire proceeding from the witnesses.
- Revelation 20:9 - fire from heaven devours the adversaries.

Ancient / Apocryphal Sources
- 1 Enoch 90 - judgment by fire upon the fallen.
- Jubilees 36 - fire as divine judgment.
- Dead Sea Scrolls (War Scroll) - fire imagery in eschatological battle.

Comparative Mythology
- Prometheus - fire as divine gift and judgment.
- Phoenix - consumed in fire, reborn in victory.
- Norse Surtr - fire giant who brings cleansing flame at Ragnarok.
- Zoroastrian Frashokereti — final purification by fire.

Modern / Scholarly Sources
- Hal Lindsey, The Late Great Planet Earth (apocalyptic fire imagery).

- Peter Levenda, Sinister Forces (ritual fire in modern occultism).
- Contemporary examples:
- Revival movements breaking out in unexpected places (fire of the Spirit).
- Atmospheric anomalies (fireballs, unexplained sky phenomena).
- Exposure and collapse of ritual abuse networks - "altars of estrangement burning."

About the Author

Drew Allen lives in East Tennessee with his wife of over 35 years and has three adult sons and (as of this writing) three grandchildren. Professionally, Drew is the founder of Atomic Cost LLC and is a seasoned consultant who has successfully served in management positions at many large and well-known companies for the nuclear, chemical process, and other industries around the world. His fraternal associations have included Master Mason of the Ancient Free and Accepted Masons (AF&AM), Order of the Knights Templar of the York Rite, Sublime Prince of the Royal Secret of the Ancient Scottish Rite, and Noble of the Ancient Arabic Order of the Nobles of the Mystic Shrine.

www.ingramcontent.com/pod-product-compliance
Lightning Source LLC
Chambersburg PA
CBHW050114280326
41933CB00010B/1102